The Historical & International Foundations of the Socialist Equality Party

This document was adopted at the
Socialist Equality Party Founding Congress
held on August 3-9, 2008.

Published on wsws.org in September & October, 2008

ISBN 978-1-893638-07-5

Published by Mehring Books
P.O. Box 48377
Oak Park, MI 48237

Printed in the United States of America

Contents

The Principled Foundations of the Socialist Equality Party 1

The Origins and Development of Marxism... 2

The Origins of Bolshevism 5

The Theory of Permanent Revolution... 8

Lenin's Defense of Materialism 10

Imperialist War and the Collapse of the Second International 13

The Russian Revolution and the Vindication of Permanent Revolution 17

The Communist International 22

The Origins of Stalinism and the Founding of the Left Opposition................... 25

The Consequences of "Socialism in One Country"... 27

The Expulsion of Trotsky 30

The Early Struggles of the International Left Opposition................................... 32

The Victory of Fascism in Germany.. 35

The Fourth International and the Struggle against Centrism 37

The Treachery of the Popular Front.. 38

The Revolution Betrayed 40

The Founding of the Fourth International 43

The Outbreak of World War II and Trotsky's Last Struggle 45

Trotsky's Defense of Materialist Dialectics 48

The Petty-Bourgeois Opposition and Party Organization.................................. 50

The Fourth International and the Outbreak of World War II.............................. 52

Trotsky's Place In History 58

The United States Enters the War... 60

The End of the War and the "Buffer States" 61

The United States and the Restabilization of Capitalism.................................... 62

The Post-war Upsurge of the Masses.. 64

The Chinese Revolution.. 65

The Establishment of Israel 67

The Korean War 68

The Origins of Pabloite Revisionism.. 69

Pablo's Repudiation of Trotskyism 72

The "Open Letter" and the Formation of the International Committee 75

The Lenin-Trotsky Theory of the Party 78

Stalinism in Crisis 79

Castroism and the SWP's Return to Pablo 80

The SLL's Defense of Trotskyism 82

The Pabloite Reunification and the Betrayal in Ceylon 84

Opposition in the SWP: The Emergence of the ACFI 85

The Third Congress of the ICFI 86

Pabloism, the New Left and Guerrillaism 88

"Continuity" vs. "Reconstruction" of the Fourth International 90

The Formation of the Workers League 91

Split in the International Committee 94

The Founding of the Workers Revolutionary Party and
    the World Crisis of 1973-75 97

Wohlforth's Break with the Workers League 98

The Workers League After Wohlforth 99

The Origins of the "Security and the Fourth International" Investigation 101

The Role of Joseph Hansen 103

A Phony "Verdict": The Pabloites Endorse the Cover-up of Stalinist Crimes 105

A Shift in the World Situation: The Capitalist Counter-Offensive 108

The Crisis in the Workers Revolutionary Party 110

The Workers League's Critique of the WRP 111

The Collapse of the WRP and the Split in the International Committee 117

A Further Comment on the Cause and Significance of the Split in the ICFI .. 122

After the Split: The Significance and Implications of Globalization 126

Perestroika and Glasnost in the USSR 130

The End of the USSR 136

The Struggle Against the Post-Soviet School of Historical Falsification 138

Globalization and the National Question 144

Globalization and the Trade Unions 147

The Formation of the Socialist Equality Party 150

The Significance of Equality 151

The World Socialist Web Site 153

The Explosion of Militarism and the Crisis of American Society 156

The Crisis of World Capitalism and
    the Tasks of the Socialist Equality Party 158

The SEP, the ICFI and the Resurgence of Marxism 162

The Historical & International Foundations of the Socialist Equality Party

The Principled Foundations of the Socialist Equality Party

1.   The program of the SEP is of a principled, not of a conjunctural and pragmatic character. It is based on an analysis of the crisis of world capitalism and an assimilation of the strategic revolutionary experiences of the working class and the international socialist movement. The world economic and political system is, in its fundamental characteristics, imperialist. Despite the advances in technology, the growth of the productive forces, and the expansion of capitalist production relations throughout the globe, the world capitalist system is beset by the same insoluble contradictions that produced the 20th century horrors of two world wars, fascism, a virtually endless series of regional military conflicts and innumerable brutal political dictatorships.

2.   The main features of imperialism identified by Lenin during World War I (the monopolistic concentration of production, the domination of finance capital and economic parasitism, the great power striving for global geo-political and economic dominance, the oppression of weaker nations, and the universal tendency toward political reaction) define the present world economic and political order. As in 1914 (on the eve of World War I) and in 1939 (on the eve of World War II), the basic contradictions are between the global economy and the nation state system, and between socialized production and private ownership of the means of production. From these contradictions emerge not only the danger of another catastrophic world war, but also the objective conditions for the overthrow of capitalism—the socialization of industry and finance, the globalization of economic life, and the social power of the working class.

1

3.   After the collapse of the Soviet Union in 1991, the ideologists and apologists of the bourgeoisie proclaimed "The End of History." By this they meant "The End of Socialism" and the final triumph of capitalism. Subsequent events have demonstrated that the obituaries for revolution, not to mention for history itself, were premature. The 21st century will be no less tumultuous than the 20th. The international working class will be confronted with the historical problems that previous generations were unable to solve.

4.   Revolutionary socialist strategy can develop only on the basis of the lessons of past struggles. Above all, the education of socialists must be directed toward developing a detailed knowledge of the history of the Fourth International. The development of Marxism as the theoretical and political spearhead of socialist revolution has found its most advanced expression in the struggles waged by the Fourth International, since its founding in 1938, against Stalinism, reformism, the Pabloite revisions of Trotskyism, and all other forms of political opportunism.

5.   Political agreement within the party on essential issues of program and tasks cannot be achieved without a common evaluation of the historical experiences of the 20th century and their central strategic lessons. Rosa Luxemburg once described history as the "Via Dolorosa" of the working class. Only to the extent that the working class learns from history—the lessons of not only its victories but also its defeats—can it be prepared for the demands of a new period of revolutionary struggle.

The Origins and Development of Marxism

6.   The imperialist epoch emerged in its modern form during the last decades of the 19th century. The expansion of capitalist industry brought with it the growth of the working class and eruption of class struggle between the bourgeoisie and the new industrial proletariat in Europe and North America. This historical process had been theoretically anticipated in the development of Marxism. *The Communist Manifesto* was published in November 1847 on the eve of the first revolutionary struggles of the working class. Through the work of Karl Marx and Friedrich Engels, utopian projects for the general improvement of the human condition were

superseded by the discovery of the objective laws governing the historical process. The materialist conception of history established, as Engels explained in his classic work *Anti-Dühring*, that:

> ...the production and, next to production, the exchange of things produced, is the basis of all social structure; that in every society that has appeared in history, the manner in which wealth is distributed and society divided into classes or estates is dependent upon what is produced, how it is produced, and how the products are exchanged. From this point of view the final causes of all social changes and political revolutions are to be sought, not in men's brains, not in man's better insight into eternal truth and justice, but in changes in the modes of production and exchange. They are to be sought, not in the philosophy, but in the economics of each particular epoch. The growing perception that existing social institutions are unreasonable and unjust, that reason has become unreason, and right wrong, is only proof that in the modes of production and exchange changes have silently taken place with which the social order, adapted to earlier economic conditions, is no longer in keeping. From this it also follows that the means of getting rid of the incongruities that have been brought to light must also be present, in a more or less developed condition, within the changed modes of production themselves. These means are not to be invented, spun out of the head, but discovered with the aid of the head in the existing material facts of production.[1]

7.   The publication of *Capital* in 1867 provided the working class with an understanding of the laws governing the capitalist mode of production. Though several years were to pass before Marx's masterwork gained the attention of a significant working class audience, *Capital* established the scientific foundation for the development of the modern socialist movement. As wider sections of the working class, especially in Germany, came under the influence of Marxism, the social and theoretical foundations emerged for the establishment of mass socialist parties throughout Europe. The

---

1   Frederick Engels, *Anti-Dühring*, in: *Marx-Engels Collected Works*, Volume 25 (New York: International Publishers, 1987), pp. 254-55.

formation of the Second International in 1889 was a milestone in the struggle for the political unity of the international working class. It rested on objective foundations far more mature, in terms of the development of capitalism and the industrial working class, than those that had existed when Marx and Engels founded the First International in 1864. The period between 1876, when the First International was dissolved, and 1889 witnessed an immense growth in capitalism and the industrial proletariat. The next quarter century was characterized by contradictory tendencies in the social, economic and political development of capitalism and the international workers' movement. On the surface, economic growth and political stability were the dominant features of the period. Within this framework, the growth of the organized workers' movement, especially in Western Europe, proceeded along parliamentary and trade union lines. However, beneath the apparent stability of the political and economic order, immense internal pressures were building up. The development of imperialism in the last decade of the 19th century and the first decade of the 20th century was accompanied by an escalation of dangerous rivalries among the major capitalist states. At the same time, economic strains were undermining the foundations of class compromise and causing an intensification of social tensions.

8.   This contradictory development underlay the tensions within the Second International, and the German Social-Democratic Party (SPD) in particular. The official doctrine of the SPD was that of class war, but its growth was bound up with the expansion of German capitalism and national industry, which brought with it the strengthening of the proletariat and the trade unions. The period of capitalist growth allowed the bourgeoisie to cultivate a section of the working class and trade union bureaucracy (what Lenin later called the "labor aristocracy"), integrating its interests with the capitalist system. This was the foundation for the growth of opportunism within the Second International, manifested in every country. This opportunism found its most developed theoretical expression in the writings of Eduard Bernstein, who rejected the Marxist analysis of the contradictions of the capitalist system and their revolutionary implications. Bernstein also rejected the scientific basis of Marxist theory, and argued that socialism should be viewed as a moral ideal that had no necessary material relationship to the laws of capitalist development.

These arguments reflected the widespread influence of various forms of subjective idealist philosophy, especially neo-Kantianism, which opposed Marxian materialism.

9.   The strength of the revisionist anti-Marxist tendencies did not reflect the intellectual power of their arguments, which were inconsistent and impressionistic. Rather, revisionism developed in a period of rapid economic expansion and rising living standards in Europe that provided the working class, though led by socialists, with no opportunity for a revolutionary assault on capitalist society. Thus, a strange dualism arose within the social-democratic movement, especially in Germany. Its leaders employed the language of revolutionary Marxism, but the daily practical work of the party proceeded within the boundaries of reformism. Bernstein's formulations reflected and justified this reformist character of the daily practice of the German Social Democratic Party and the trade unions. The political implications of his theoretical revisions found expression in France, in 1899, when the socialist leader Millerand became a minister in a bourgeois government.

The Origins of Bolshevism

10.   The Bolshevik tendency emerged out of the struggle led politically by Lenin (and, in the sphere of philosophy, by Plekhanov) against revisionist and opportunist tendencies within the Russian Social Democratic Labor Party. Lenin (basing himself on the position developed earlier by Kautsky, the principal theoretician of the SPD) insisted that socialist consciousness did not develop spontaneously within the working class, but had to be brought into the workers' movement. In his seminal work, *What Is To Be Done?* Lenin cited the following critical passage from the program of the Austrian Social-Democratic Party:

> ...Modern socialist consciousness can only arise on the basis of profound scientific knowledge. Indeed, modern economic science is as much a condition for socialist production as, say, modern technology, and the proletariat can create neither the one nor the other, no matter how much it may desire to do so; both arise out of the

modern social process. The vehicle of science is not the proletariat, but the bourgeois intelligentsia: it was in the minds of individual members of this stratum that modern socialism originated, and it was they who communicated it to the more intellectually developed proletarians who, in their turn, introduce it into the proletarian class struggle where conditions allow this to be done. Thus, socialist consciousness is something introduced into the proletarian class struggle from without, and not something that arose within it spontaneously.[2]

11.   The central task of the revolutionary party was to saturate the workers' movement with Marxist theory. "Since there can be no talk of an independent ideology formulated by the working masses themselves in the process of their movement," Lenin wrote, "the only choice is—either bourgeois or socialist ideology. There is no middle course (for mankind has not created a 'third' ideology, and, moreover, in a society torn by class antagonisms there can never be a non-class or an above-class ideology.) Hence, to belittle the socialist ideology in any way, to turn aside from it in the slightest degree means to strengthen bourgeois ideology."[3] Lenin opposed all tendencies that adapted their work to the spontaneous forms of working class activity and detached the daily practical struggles from the historical goal of social revolution. Lenin recognized more clearly than any other socialist of his time that the development of Marxism within the working class required a persistent struggle against the political and ideological pressure exerted by bourgeois and middle class tendencies. Herein lay the significance of the fight—conducted over issues of theory, political strategy and party organization—against diverse forms of revisionism and opportunism.

12.   The 1903 Second Congress of the Russian Social-Democratic Labor Party ended in a split between the Bolshevik and Menshevik tendencies. It marked a turning point in the history of the revolutionary socialist movement. Though the split occurred unexpectedly, over what at

2   "What Is To Be Done?" in: V. I. Lenin, *Collected Works*, Volume 5, (Moscow: Foreign Languages Publishing House, 1961), pp. 383-84.

3   Ibid., p. 384.

first seemed to be secondary issues relating to party rules and organization, it gradually became clear that the conflict was tied to the larger problem of political opportunism in the RSDLP and, beyond that, to issues of political perspective and program. In relation to the organizational question, as Lenin explained in *One Step Forward, Two Steps Back*, "Opportunism in program is naturally connected with opportunism in tactics and opportunism in organization."[4] He noted further, "The opportunist wing of any party always defends and justifies all backwardness, whether in program, tactics or organization."[5] Lenin concluded his analysis with a memorable declaration:

> In its struggle for power the proletariat has no other weapon but organization. Disunited by the rule of anarchic competition in the bourgeois world, ground down by forced labor for capital, constantly thrust back to the "lower depths" of utter destitution, savagery, and degeneration, the proletariat can, and inevitably will, become an invincible force only through its ideological unification on the principles of Marxism being reinforced by the material unity of organization, which welds millions of toilers into an army of the working class.[6]

13.   Following the Second Congress, Lenin's uncompromising stance came under bitter criticism within many sections of the RSDLP that held him responsible for the split. His approach to the inner-party struggle was harshly criticized by the young Trotsky (who was only 23 at the time of the Congress) and Rosa Luxemburg. These outstanding revolutionists did not yet understand Lenin's insight into the material relationship between theoretical, political and organizational disputes within the party and the objective social process of class realignments and class conflict developing on a mass scale outside the party. While most socialists of the day tended to interpret the conflict within and between factions of the RSDLP as a

---

4   "One Step Forward, Two Steps Back" in: V. I. Lenin, *Collected Works*, Volume 7 (Moscow: Progress Publishers, 1965), p. 398.

5   Ibid., p. 395.

6   Ibid., p. 415.

conflict of tendencies competing, in a subjective sense, for influence over a politically uncommitted working class, Lenin interpreted the conflict as an objective manifestation of real shifts in class relations—both between the working class and the bourgeoisie and also between different strata within the working class itself. Lenin studied the struggle of tendencies within the party as a "key indicator" of the development of the revolutionary epoch. In relation to the conflict that erupted at the Second Congress, the issue concealed within the constitutional question was the relationship of the Russian working class and the RSDLP to the liberal bourgeoisie and its political parties. Underlying the opportunist attitude of the Mensheviks toward organizational issues, such as the definition of the responsibilities of party membership, was a conciliatory orientation toward Russian liberalism. Over time, as the political situation in Russia matured, the immense implications of the organizational issues became more apparent. As Trotsky later acknowledged, his understanding of Lenin's political methods deepened as, against the backdrop of cataclysmic events, he "worked out a more and more correct, i.e., Bolshevik, conception of the relations between class and party, between theory and politics, and between politics and organization...What had seemed to me to be 'splitterism,' 'disruption,' etc., now appeared as a salutary and incomparably farsighted struggle for the revolutionary independence of the proletarian party."[7]

The Theory of Permanent Revolution

14.   The split at the 1903 Congress anticipated social upheaval in Russia. The Russian Revolution of 1905 raised crucial problems of strategy for Russian Social Democracy. Despite the defeat of the revolution, the events of 1905 demonstrated the immense social power of the working class, which played the leading role in the struggle against the tsarist regime. Prior to 1905, revolutions were seen as national events, the outcomes of which were determined by the logic of their internal socio-economic structures and relations. Marxist theoreticians had assumed that the socialist

---

7   "Our Differences," in *The Challenge of the Left Opposition (1923-25)* [New York: Pathfinder Press, 2002), p. 299.

revolution would begin in the most advanced European capitalist countries (Britain, Germany and France), and that the less developed countries (such as Russia), would have to pass through an extended stage of capitalist economic and bourgeois-democratic political development before they were "ripe" for a proletarian socialist revolution. In the latter countries, it was generally maintained that Marxist parties would be obligated to limit the revolutionary struggle to the establishment of a democratic republic under the political leadership of the national bourgeoisie. This traditional perspective guided the work of the Russian Mensheviks, following the political strategy developed by Plekhanov. In the 1905 revolution, however, the bourgeoisie proved unwilling to carry through the democratic revolution against the Tsar, and instead sided with the Tsar against the working class.

15.   Lenin, in opposition to the Mensheviks, argued that because of the political weakness of the bourgeoisie, the revolution would be led by the working class in alliance with the peasantry. This alliance would establish a "democratic dictatorship of the proletariat and peasantry." This formulation expressed Lenin's determination to impart to the democratic revolution the most radical character possible (i.e., the uncompromising destruction of all remnants of feudal relations in the countryside and the resolute destruction of autocratic rule). But it did not define in socialist terms either the revolution or the state that was to issue from it. The democratic dictatorship did not necessitate an encroachment on bourgeois capitalist property. Moreover, it remained ambiguous on the distribution of power between the proletariat and peasantry.

16.   Trotsky's Theory of Permanent Revolution presented a bolder solution to the problem of the democratic revolution in Russia. His conception was without the ambiguity, relating to the class nature of the state power that would issue from the overthrow of tsarism, which characterized Lenin's formulation. Trotsky predicted that the revolution would not be limited to democratic tasks, that it would assume a socialist character, and that the working class would take state power and establish its dictatorship. The nature, tasks and outcome of the Russian revolution, Trotsky insisted, would be determined by international rather than national conditions. Though the immediate tasks that confronted the Russian masses were of a bourgeois-democratic character—the overthrow of the tsarist

autocracy and the liquidation of the remnants of feudal relations in the countryside—they could not be realized either under the political leadership of the national bourgeoisie or within the framework of a bourgeois-democratic republic. The changes in world economy and the emergence of the working class as a powerful social force meant that the democratic revolution in the 20th century would develop very differently than in the 19th. The Russian bourgeoisie, having been integrated into the world capitalist system, was weak and dependent upon imperialism. The democratic tasks could be realized only through a revolution led by the working class with the support of the peasant masses. Having taken power, however, the working class could not limit itself to democratic tasks and would be compelled to carry out measures of a socialist character. Moreover, the social revolution in Russia could not maintain itself within a national framework. Its survival depended upon the extension of the revolution into the advanced capitalist countries and, ultimately, throughout the world. Trotsky wrote in June 1905:

> Binding all countries together with its mode of production and its commerce, capitalism has converted the whole world into a single economic and political organism...This immediately gives the events now unfolding an international character, and opens up a wide horizon. The political emancipation of Russia led by the working class will raise that class to a height as yet unknown in history, will transfer to it colossal power and resources, and make it the initiator of the liquidation of world capitalism, for which history has created all the objective conditions.[8]

Lenin's Defense of Materialism

17.   In later years, Trotsky commented that Lenin's work was distinguished by the highest level of theoretical conscientiousness. This found particular expression in Lenin's defense of Marxism against different forms of philosophical idealism and subjectivism that threatened to disorient the

---

8   Leon Trotsky, *The Permanent Revolution* (London: New Park, 1971), pp. 239-40.

socialist movement. Lenin's decision to devote an entire year to the writing of *Materialism and Empirio-Criticism* (1908-09) reflected his awareness of the immense danger posed by the widespread influence of philosophical idealism within the socialist movement, not only neo-Kantianism— often associated with efforts to base socialism on ethics—but also openly irrationalist conceptions, expressing the influence of Schopenhauer and Nietzsche, which glorified voluntarism and the subjective will to action. Lenin opposed idealist subjectivism as incompatible with a scientific understanding of the laws governing capitalist society and the revolutionary struggle.

18.   Lenin insisted, "The philosophy of Marxism is materialism." He stated that materialism "has proved to be the only philosophy that is consistent, true to all the teachings of natural science and hostile to superstition, cant and so forth." He explained that Marxism had developed materialism beyond the form in which it existed in the 18th century, by enriching it "with the achievements of German classical philosophy, especially of Hegel's system, which in its turn had led to the materialism of Feuerbach." The great contribution of German classical philosophy was the elaboration of dialectics, defined by Lenin as "the doctrine of development in its fullest, deepest and most comprehensive form, the doctrine of the relativity of human knowledge that provides us with a reflection of eternally developing matter."[9] Writing on the eve of World War I, Lenin provided this concise explanation of the philosophical standpoint of Marxism:

> Marx deepened and developed philosophical materialism to the full, and extended the cognition of nature to include the cognition of human society. His historical materialism was a great achievement in scientific thinking. The chaos and arbitrariness that had previously reigned in views on history and politics were replaced by a strikingly integral and harmonious scientific theory, which shows how, in consequence of the growth of the productive forces, out of one system of social life another and higher system develops—how capitalism, for instance, grows out of feudalism.

---

9   "Three Sources and Three Component Parts of Marxism," in V. I. Lenin, *Collected Works*, Volume 19 (Moscow: Progress Publishers, 1968), p. 24.

Just as man's knowledge reflects nature (i.e., developing matter), which exists independently of him, so man's social knowledge (i.e., his various views and doctrines—philosophical, religious, political and so forth) reflects the economic system of society. Political institutions are a superstructure on the economic foundation. We see, for example, that the various political forms of the modern European states serve to strengthen the domination of the bourgeoisie over the proletariat.

Marx's philosophy is a consummate philosophical materialism which has provided mankind, and especially the working class, with powerful instruments of knowledge.[10]

19.   After the publication of Georg Lukács' *History and Class Consciousness* in 1922, numerous efforts were made by academically-trained intellectuals, schooled in idealist philosophy, within and on the periphery of the socialist movement, to counterpose dialectics to materialism; and even to discredit works such as *Materialism and Empirio-Criticism* as examples of a "vulgar materialism" that Lenin supposedly repudiated once he undertook a systematic study of Hegel's *Science of Logic* in 1914-15. Such claims, which were (and continue to be) based on a gross distortion of not only Lenin's *Philosophical Notebooks* but also of his intellectual biography, played a major role in the bourgeois assault on the foundations and heritage of classical Marxism that gathered strength against the backdrop of the triumph of Stalinism in the USSR, the rise of fascism in Germany, and the physical liquidation of large sections of the theoretically-educated revolutionary cadre of Europe. The "dialectic" to which the idealists paid a purely rhetorical tribute has nothing whatsoever to do with the "doctrine of development" referred to by Lenin, let alone with the genuinely scientific method, described by Engels, which "comprehends things and their representations, ideas, in their essential connection, concatenation, motion, origin, and ending."[11] It was, rather, a "dialectic" from which nature, the material universe existing prior to and independent of man, was excluded. It was (and is) the pseudo-dialectic of a subjectively-conceived interaction

---

10 Ibid., p. 25.

11 *Anti-Dühring*, in: *Marx-Engels Collected Works*, Volume 25, p. 23.

of the discontented petty-bourgeois intellectual and his environment, in which that individual—unbound by objective laws that govern the development of nature, society and consciousness—is free to "create" the world as he or she sees fit.

Imperialist War and the Collapse of the Second International

20.   The tensions building up in world capitalism erupted in the First World War, which, with all its horrors, announced the opening of the epoch of the "death agony of capitalism" and of the world socialist revolution. As early as the 1880s, Engels had warned of the consequences of capitalist militarism and the danger of war. Prior to 1914, at a series of Congresses, the Second International had issued manifestos calling on the working class to resist the outbreak of war, and, if a war broke out, to utilize the crisis to "rouse the people and hasten the downfall of capitalism." However, the assassination of the Austrian Archduke Franz Ferdinand on June 28, 1914—the spark that set off long-standing conflicts within the bourgeoisie of Europe—revealed overnight the implications of the growth of opportunism within the socialist movement. On August 4, 1914, the representatives of the SPD voted to financially support the war, and almost all the major parties of the International fell in line behind the war policies of their bourgeois governments.

21.   In opposition to the capitulation of the Second International, the Bolshevik Party, under the leadership of Lenin, came out against the war. Within weeks of its outbreak, Lenin authored a resolution that defined the conflict as "a bourgeois, imperialist and dynastic war." The resolution declared:

> "The conduct of the leaders of the German Social-Democratic Party, the strongest and most influential in the Second International (1889-1914), a party which has voted for war credits and repeated the bourgeois-chauvinist phrases of the Prussian Junkers and the bourgeoisie, is sheer betrayal of socialism. Under no circumstances can the conduct of the leaders of the German Social-Democratic Party be condoned, even if we assume that the party was absolutely weak and

had temporarily to bow to the will of the bourgeois majority of the nation. This party has in fact adopted a national-liberal policy."[12]

22.   The resolution condemned the actions of the French and Belgian socialist parties as "just as reprehensible."[13] It proceeded to place the tragic events of August 1914 in the necessary political and historical context:

> The betrayal of socialism by most leaders of the Second International (1889-1914) signifies the ideological and political bankruptcy of the International. This collapse has been mainly caused by the actual prevalence in it of petty-bourgeois opportunism, the bourgeois nature and danger of which have long been indicated by the finest representatives of the revolutionary proletariat of all countries. The opportunists had long been preparing to wreck the Second International by denying the socialist revolution and substituting bourgeois reformism in its stead, by rejecting the class struggle with its inevitable conversion at certain moments into civil war, and by preaching class collaboration; by preaching bourgeois chauvinism under the guise of patriotism and the defense of the fatherland, and ignoring or rejecting the fundamental truth of socialism, long ago set forth in the *Communist Manifesto*, that the workingmen have no country; by confining themselves, in the struggle against militarism, to a sentimental philistine point of view, instead of recognizing the need for a revolutionary war by the proletarians of all countries, against the bourgeoisie of all countries; by making a fetish of the necessary utilization of parliamentarianism and bourgeois legality, and forgetting that illegal forms of organization and agitation are imperative at times of crises.[14]

23.   Lenin insisted that the capitulation of the Second International meant the political death of that organization as an instrument of revolu-

---

12   "The Tasks of Revolutionary Social-Democracy in the European War," in: V.I. Lenin, *Collected Works*, Volume 21 (Moscow: Progress Publishers, 1974), p. 16.

13   Ibid., p. 16.

14   Ibid., pp. 16-17.

tionary struggle. It was, therefore, necessary to proceed with the construction of a new, Third International. This new International had to be based on an uncompromising struggle against opportunism, which had revealed itself in August 1914 as an agency of imperialism within the international workers' movement. Lenin rejected any explanation of the collapse of the Second International that trivialized the event by treating it as if it were the product of individual mistakes and weaknesses. "At all events," Lenin wrote, "it is absurd to substitute the question of the role of individuals for the question of the struggle between trends and of the new period in the working class movement."[15] As Lenin anticipated, the division between Marxism and opportunism precipitated a fundamental realignment of the workers movement, reflected in every country, between national chauvinist and international tendencies. It was out of this division that the new Communist Parties would later emerge.

24.   World War I had deep roots in the development of capitalism, and in particular the contradiction between an increasingly global economy and the capitalist nation-state system. Trotsky wrote in 1915, "The present war is at bottom a revolt of the forces of production against the political form of nation and state. It means the collapse of the national state as an independent economic unit...The War of 1914 is the most colossal breakdown in history of an economic system destroyed by its own inherent contradictions."[16] This meant at the same time that the old Social-Democratic Parties, which had developed in a period of stupendous growth of national economies, were shaken to their core by the breakdown of the familiar conditions that had shaped their political routines over several decades. The formal theoretical and rhetorical defense of the revolutionary perspective had been balanced with a practice that was of a predominantly reformist character. But the change of conditions made the continuation of political and theoretical double bookkeeping impossible. "In their historic crash the national states have pulled down with them the national Socialist parties also...As the national states have become a hindrance to the development of the forces of production, so the old Socialist

---

15 "The Collapse of the Second International," Ibid., p. 250.

16 Leon Trotsky, *War and the International* (Young Socialist Publications, 1971), p. vii-viii.

parties have become the main hindrance to the revolutionary movement of the working class."[17]

25.   Seeking the source of opportunism within the Second International, Lenin analyzed the economic and social-political changes in the structure of world capitalism associated with the emergence of imperialism. Criticizing the formulations of Karl Kautsky, the theoretical leader of German Social Democracy who had capitulated to the opportunists in August 1914, Lenin rejected the latter's claim that imperialism was merely a "preferred" policy. Rather, Lenin explained:

> ...Imperialism is a specific historical stage of capitalism. Its specific character is threefold: Imperialism is (1) monopoly capitalism; (2) parasitic, or decaying capitalism; (3) moribund capitalism. The supplanting of free competition by monopoly is the fundamental economic feature, the quintessence of imperialism.[18]

26.   Lenin also rejected Kautsky's theory of "ultra-imperialism," which hypothesized the possibility of the peaceful, non-violent, non-imperialist regulation of world economy and the relations between the major capitalist powers:

> ...The essence of the matter [Lenin wrote] is that Kautsky detaches the politics of imperialism from its economics, speaks of annexations as being a policy "preferred" by finance capital, and opposes to it another bourgeois policy which, he alleges, is possible on this very same basis of finance capital. It follows, then, that monopolies in the economy are compatible with non-monopolistic, non-violent, non-annexationist methods in politics. It follows, then, that the territorial division of the world, which was completed during this very epoch of finance capital, and which constitutes the basis of the present peculiar forms of rivalry between the biggest capitalist states, is compatible with a non-imperialist policy. The result is a

---

17   Ibid., p. xii-xiii.

18   "Imperialism and the Split in Socialism," in: V.I. Lenin, *Collected Works*, Volume 23, p. 105.

slurring-over and a blunting of the most profound contradictions of the latest stage of capitalism, instead of an exposure of their depth; the result is bourgeois reformism instead of Marxism.[19]

The Russian Revolution and the Vindication of Permanent Revolution

27.   Between 1914 and 1917 Lenin and Trotsky foresaw that the imperialist war would set the stage for revolutionary eruptions in Europe. This perspective was vindicated with the outbreak of the February Revolution, which arose out of the war and its extreme exacerbation of the crisis of Russian society. After the February Revolution of 1917 overthrew the Tsar, the Mensheviks sided with the bourgeois Provisional Government and opposed a revolution of the working class. The Provisional Government defended capitalist property relations, continued to prosecute the war, and opposed the distribution of land to the peasantry. Lenin returned to Russia in April and, repudiating in practice the longstanding Bolshevik program of the democratic dictatorship, called for the working class to oppose the Provisional Government and take power through the Soviets. This position validated and endorsed, in all essentials, Trotsky's Theory of Permanent Revolution, which had, to an extraordinary degree, anticipated the actual course of revolutionary developments and laid the foundations, theoretically and politically, for Lenin's decisive reorientation of the Bolshevik Party in April 1917. Lenin's adoption of Trotsky's perspective was bitterly opposed by many "Old Bolsheviks," including Stalin. Prior to Lenin's return to Russia in April 1917, the position taken by Stalin, as editor of *Pravda*, the Bolshevik newspaper, was that critical support should be given to the Provisional government. He also advocated support for the continuation of the war effort.

28.   In the months leading up to the overthrow of the bourgeois Provisional Government, Lenin undertook an extensive study of the writings of Marx and Engels on the subject of the state. This work answered

---

19 "Imperialism, The Highest Stage of Capitalism," in: V. I. Lenin, *Collected Works*, Volume 22, p. 270.

the opportunists who were striving to portray the state as a supra-class institution, which existed to reconcile and arbitrate differences between classes. Lenin called attention to Engels's definition of the state as a co-ercive instrument employed by the bourgeoisie to defend its rule, and to oppress and exploit the working class. This definition, Lenin argued, had lost none of its relevance in the 20th century. On the contrary:

> Imperialism—the era of bank capital, the era of gigantic capital-ist monopolies, of the development of monopoly capitalism into state-monopoly capitalism—has clearly shown an extraordinary strengthening of the "state machine" and an unprecedented growth in its bureaucratic and military apparatus in connection with the intensification of repressive measures against the proletariat both in the monarchical and in the freest, republican countries.[20]

29.   In October 1917, the Bolsheviks, having won the majority in the Petrograd Soviet, organized an insurrection under the leadership of Trotsky, overthrew the Provisional Government and transferred power to the Soviets. Serious historical research has refuted claims that the October Revolution was a conspiratorial "putsch" undertaken by the Bolsheviks without mass support.[21] In fact, there existed overwhelming support in the working class of Petrograd, the Russian capital, for the overthrow of the bourgeois regime. However, within the Bolshevik leadership there was sub-stantial opposition. Lev Kamenev and Grigory Zinoviev, who were among Lenin's closest collaborators, were convinced that an insurrection would meet with disaster. They anticipated insurmountable obstacles to the vic-tory of the revolution. They stressed the still substantial military forces commanded by Kerensky, the leader of the Provisional Government, and the artillery that was deployed around the capital. As it turned out, the cal-culations of the Bolshevik opponents of insurrection were far off the mark. The overthrow of the Provisional Government was achieved with remark-able ease, and with very little bloodshed. Trotsky, commenting later on the

---

20 "The State and Revolution," in: V. I. Lenin, *Collected Works*, Volume 25, p. 410.

21 See Professor Alexander Rabinowitch's *The Bolsheviks in Power* (Bloomfield: Indiana University Press, 2007).

significance of the struggle within the Bolshevik Party that preceded the insurrection, noted:

> ...there are two types of leaders who incline to drag the party back at the very moment when it must take a stupendous leap forward. Some among them generally tend to see mainly the difficulties and obstacles in the way of revolution, and to estimate each situation with a preconceived, though not always conscious, intention of avoiding any action. Marxism in their hands is turned into a method for establishing the impossibility of revolutionary action. The purest specimens of this type are the Russian Mensheviks. But this type as such is not confined to Menshevism, and at the most critical movement it suddenly manifests itself in responsible posts in the most revolutionary party.
>
> The representatives of the second variety are distinguished by their superficial and agitational approach. They never see any obstacles or difficulties until they come into a head-on collision with them. The capacity for surmounting real obstacles by means of bombastic phrases, the tendency to evince lofty optimism on all questions ("the ocean is only knee deep"), is inevitably transformed into its polar opposite when the hour for decisive action strikes. To the first type of revolutionist, who makes mountains out of molehills, the problems of seizing power lie in heaping up and multiplying to the nth degree all the difficulties he has become accustomed to see in his way. To the second type, the superficial optimist, the difficulties of revolutionary action always come as a surprise. In the preparatory period the behavior of the two is different: the former is a skeptic, upon whom one cannot rely too much, that is, in a revolutionary sense; the latter, on the contrary, may seem a fanatic revolutionist. But at the decisive moment, the two march hand in hand; they both oppose the insurrection.[22]

30.   The Russian Revolution provided an impulse for upheavals throughout the world. The revolutionary government called for an end

---

22 "Lessons of October," by Leon Trotsky, in *The Challenge of the Left Opposition 1923-25* (New York: Pathfinder Press, 2002), pp. 286-87.

to the war, released secret treaties exposing the imperialist designs of the belligerents, and urged workers to rise up against their governments. The Mensheviks remained intransigent in their opposition to the overthrow of the Provisional Government, despite the fact that the Bolshevik-led revolution clearly enjoyed mass support. Even after the overthrow, the Mensheviks rebuffed efforts of moderate Bolsheviks such as Kamenev to draw them into a socialist coalition government. The Mensheviks insisted that their price for any collaboration with the Bolsheviks was not only the removal of Lenin and Trotsky from any positions of power but also having them handed over to police authorities!

31.   The failure of the Bolshevik Party to come to power could only have led to a counter-revolution, resulting in the restoration of the Tsar or the establishment of a military dictatorship. Once the bourgeoisie and its imperialist patrons recovered from their initial shock, they instigated a civil war with the aim of destroying the revolutionary regime. The Red Army was formed, under the leadership of Trotsky, to defend the Soviet regime against counterrevolution. Trotsky proved to be a military strategist and organizer of genius. His success as the leader of the Red Army reflected his incomparable understanding of the objective tasks confronting the working class and his ability to convey that understanding to the masses. In a speech delivered in April 1918, Trotsky explained:

> History is no indulgent, soft mother who will protect the working class: she is a wicked stepmother who will teach the workers through bloody experience how they must attain their aims. The working people are readily inclined to forgive and forget: it is enough for the conditions of struggle to have become a little easier, enough for them to have won something, for it to seem to them that the main job has been done, and they are disposed to show magnanimity, to become passive, to stop fighting. In this lies the misfortune of the working people. But the possessing classes never give up the struggle. They have been educated to offer constant opposition to the pressure of the working masses, and any passivity, indecision, or wavering on our part results in our exposing our weak spot to blows of the possessing classes so that tomorrow or the next day they inevitably launch a new onslaught upon us. The working class needs not the

universal forgiveness that Tolstoy preached, but hard tempering, intransigence, profound conviction that without struggle for every step, every inch of the road leading to betterment of its life, without constant, irreconcilable harsh struggle, and without organization of this struggle, there can be no salvation and liberation.[23]

32. The Bolsheviks were convinced that the fate of the Russian Revolution depended upon the extension of the revolution beyond the borders of Soviet Russia. This position was held by the finest representatives of international socialism. Defending the Bolsheviks, Rosa Luxemburg wrote, "Lenin and Trotsky and their friends were the first, those who went ahead as an example to the proletariat of the world; they are still the only ones up to now who can cry with Hutten: 'I have dared!'" The Russian Revolution transformed the question of socialism from a purely theoretical into a practical question. However, Luxemburg insisted that the fate of the Russian Revolution depended on the outcome of the class struggle beyond the borders of Russia. "In Russia the problem could only be posed," she wrote. "It could not be solved in Russia. And in this sense, the future everywhere belongs to 'Bolshevism.'"[24] The bourgeoisie saw in the emerging revolutionary movements its most dangerous opponents. The combined forces of world imperialism organized an intervention in Russia in support of counter-revolution. In Germany, the forces of reaction, in league with the Social Democrats who had been raised to power by the working class uprising of November 1918, organized in January 1919 the murder of Rosa Luxemburg and Karl Liebknecht. The assassination of these two revolutionary leaders was the political response of the German (and world) bourgeoisie to the Russian Revolution. The ruling classes had concluded from 1917 that the development of Marxist leadership in the working class had to be prevented at all costs. The bloody events of the 20th century would demonstrate the extent to which the ruling classes and their agents among the Social Democrats and Stalinists were guided by this lesson.

---

23 *How the Revolution Armed: The Military Writings and Speeches of Leon Trotsky*, Volume 1: 1918, Translated by Brian Pearce (London: New Park Publications, 1979), p. 58.

24 *The Russian Revolution* (Ann Arbor: University of Michigan Press, 1961), p. 80.

The Communist International

33.   The Third International, or Communist International (Comintern), held its first Congress in Moscow in March 1919. The Soviet Republic was still defending itself against imperialist-backed counter-revolutionary forces. Under siege conditions, the Communist International elaborated the program, strategy and tactics for world revolution as a practical task confronting the international working class. Drawing on the tragic lessons of 1914, the Communist International was to be based on an uncompromising struggle against opportunism and revisionism, which had led to the demise of the Second International. On July 30, 1920, Trotsky introduced the *Theses on the Conditions of Admission to the Communist International*, which enumerated the so-called "21 Points" defining the terms of membership in the international revolutionary organization. Parties seeking membership in the Comintern would be obligated to "regularly and methodically remove reformists and centrists from every responsible post in the labor movement," and recognize "the necessity of a complete break with reformism and 'centrist' politics…"[25]

34.   Trotsky explained that the Comintern was established as a "school of revolutionary strategy" that would oversee the development of new Communist Parties around the world, based on an understanding of the objective situation, the elaboration of correct tactics, and the fight against opportunism. He wrote, "The task of the working class—in Europe and throughout the world—consists in counterposing to the thoroughly thought-out counter-revolutionary strategy of the bourgeoisie its own revolutionary strategy, likewise thought out to the end. For this it is first of all necessary to understand that it will not be possible to overthrow the bourgeoisie automatically, mechanically, merely because it is condemned by history."[26]

35.   At the end of World War I, the extension of revolution was an imminent possibility. In November 1918, the outbreak of revolution in

---

25 *Theses, Resolutions and Manifestos of the First Four Congresses of the Third International* [London: Inks Links, 1980] pp. 93-94.

26 *The First Five Years of the Communist International*, Volume Two (London: New Park, 1974), p. 7.

Germany led quickly to the abdication of the Kaiser and the proclamation
of a republic. Political power fell into the hands of the SPD, which did everything it could to strangle the revolution. In contradistinction to Russia
18 months earlier, there did not exist in Germany a developed political
party tempered by years of intransigent struggle against revisionism and
centrism. The left-wing opponents of the SPD had hesitated far too long in
proceeding to a decisive organizational break with the Social-Democratic
Party. A substantial faction of that opposition situated itself halfway between the SPD and Bolshevism. It was not until late December 1918 that
the most revolutionary faction in Germany, the Spartacists, proceeded to
found the Communist Party. Then, in January 1919, with little preparation
and with no strategic plan, an insurrection broke out in Berlin. The SPD
regime mobilized right-wing shock troops to suppress the uprising and
sanctioned the murder of Rosa Luxemburg and Karl Liebknecht.

36.   Further defeats of the insurgent working class in Europe followed. In March 1921, a premature and ill-prepared insurrection was suppressed by the German state. At the Third Congress of the Communist
International in 1921, Lenin and Trotsky intervened decisively against
"ultra-leftism." Communist parties, they insisted, could not conquer power
without first winning the support of the masses. A pamphlet written
by Lenin, entitled *"Left-Wing" Communism—An Infantile Disorder*, was
distributed to the Congress delegates. It pointed out that the Bolshevik
Party developed in struggle not only against Menshevism, but also "against
petty-bourgeois revolutionism, which smacks of anarchism, or borrows
something from the latter and, in all essential matters, does not measure
up to the conditions and requirements of a consistently proletarian class
struggle."[27]

37.   Lenin explained that the Bolshevik victory in October 1917
would not have been possible if the revolutionary party had not previously
engaged in, and mastered, many forms of political struggle. He refuted
radical shibboleths that rejected, under all conditions, political compromises, denied the legitimacy of engaging in electoral and parliamentary
activity, and declared it impermissible to work inside reactionary trade

---

27 *"Left-Wing" Communism—An Infantile Disorder*, in: V. I. Lenin, *Collected Works*,
Volume 31 (Moscow: Progress Publishers, 1966), p. 32.

unions. The Third Congress counseled Communist parties to prepare for a more prolonged period in which they would have to win over the allegiance of the working class. Among the tactical initiatives encouraged by Lenin and Trotsky was the utilization of the demand for a "united front" of mass working class organizations. The purpose of the "united front" was to organize the defense of the working class, or to undertake the struggle for important demands in a manner that demonstrated to the masses both the revolutionary initiative of the Communist parties and the perfidy of the Social Democrats. The aim of the united front was not to declare a political amnesty and refrain from criticizing political opponents. Rather, the tactic sought to realize the objective need of the working class for unity in struggle, while at the same time raising its political consciousness by exposing its opportunist leaderships.

38.   The shift in political course implemented at the Third Congress brought substantial gains. Especially in Germany, the authority of the Communist Party increased significantly. But in early 1923, the political situation changed dramatically. The devastating collapse of the German economy in the early spring, followed by unprecedented inflation, set into motion a process that seemed to be leading inexorably to the revolutionary overthrow of the bourgeois state. The membership of the discredited SPD melted away, while that of the Communist Party (the KPD) grew rapidly. By October 1923 the conditions for a successful revolution appeared extraordinarily favorable. A date was set for the insurrection, October 25—the sixth anniversary of the Soviet revolution. Then, at the last moment, Heinrich Brandler, the leader of the KPD, cancelled the scheduled insurrection. State forces quickly suppressed isolated insurgent activity in cities where local leaders had not learned of the decision to call the insurrection off. Instead of a socialist revolution, the German October ended in a political fiasco.

39.   For Trotsky, the failure of the German Revolution in 1923 was a demonstration in the negative of the supreme political truth: given the existence of the necessary objective conditions for revolution, the subjective factor of leadership assumes decisive significance in the struggle for power. Moreover, he noted that historical experience had demonstrated that the transition to the struggle for power invariably provokes within the revolutionary party a severe political crisis. Such crises have immense

significance, and how they are resolved is likely to determine the f; revolution for years, if not decades. Trotsky wrote:

> A revolutionary party is subjected to the pressure of other political forces. At every given stage of its development the party elaborates its own methods of counteracting and resisting this pressure. During a tactical turn and the resulting internal regroupments and frictions, the party's power of resistance becomes weakened. From this the possibility always arises that the internal groupings in the party, which originate from the necessity of a turn in tactics, may develop far beyond the original controversial points of departure and serve as a support for various class tendencies. To put the case more plainly: the party that does not keep step with the historical tasks of its own class becomes, or runs the risk of becoming, the indirect tool of other classes.[28]

The Origins of Stalinism and the Founding of the Left Opposition

40.   The defeat of the German revolution of 1923 contributed to strengthening conservative tendencies in the Soviet state and Communist Party bureaucracies. These tendencies grew further after the Soviet regime implemented the New Economic Policy in the spring of 1921. The NEP sanctioned a revival of the capitalist market, and significant economic concessions to capitalist strata in the city and countryside. The aim of these concessions was to revive economic activity, which had been shattered by years of war and revolution. While Lenin and Trotsky had hoped that the NEP would be a relatively short-term policy—to buy time for the Soviet Union until a renewed upsurge of international revolutionary struggle—it strengthened conservative social forces and changed the economic and political dynamic of Soviet life. These processes were reflected in the Bolshevik Party and undermined Trotsky's position in the leadership. Within the ruling strata and the rapidly expanding ranks of

---

28 "Lessons of October," in: Challenge of the Left Opposition, pp. 228-29.

the party and state bureaucracy, moods of conservatism and complacency began to find ever-more open political expression. As Trotsky recalled in his autobiography:

> ... The sentiment of "Not all and always for the revolution, but something for oneself as well," was translated as "Down with permanent revolution." The revolt against the exacting theoretical demands of Marxism and the exacting political demands of the revolution gradually assumed, in the eyes of these people, the form of a struggle against "Trotskyism." Under this banner, the liberation of the philistine in the Bolshevik was proceeding. It was because of this that I lost power, and it was this that determined the form which this loss took.[29]

41.   The attacks on Leon Trotsky and the Theory of Permanent Revolution—initiated with the lie that "Trotsky underestimates the peasantry"—were the political reflection of the hostility of the state and party bureaucracy to the internationalist program of the October Revolution. The growing political power of Stalin, and the bureaucratic dictatorship with which his name is associated, was not an inevitable product of socialist revolution, but developed out of contradictions specific to a workers' state established in a backward country and isolated by the defeats of the international revolution. The legacy of economic backwardness inherited from tsarist Russia was compounded by the disastrous consequences of seven years of imperialist war (1914-17) and civil war (1918-21). These conditions imposed immense burdens on the effort of the Bolshevik regime to build the Soviet economy. Moreover, the civil war had exacted an enormous human toll on the working class and the Bolshevik Party itself. Tens of thousands of class-conscious workers, who had formed the basis of the popular support for the Bolshevik seizure of power, had been killed. Another major factor in the degeneration of the Bolshevik Party was the integration of a substantial portion of its cadre into the burgeoning state and party bureaucracy. Long-time revolutionists were transformed into administrators, and this change had, over time, an impact on their political orientation. Moreover, the demands of the new state for capable administrators required the recruitment

---

29 Leon Trotsky, *My Life* (New York: Charles Scribner's Sons, 1931), p. 505.

of many people who had served before 1917 in the bureaucracy of the old regime. These cumulative changes in the state structure, the social function of many "Old" Bolsheviks, and the overall position of the working class ultimately found political expression.

42.   As Trotsky explained, the Soviet state that emerged from revolution and civil war was a highly contradictory phenomenon. As the product of a genuine working class revolution, the new state rested upon, and defended, new property relations, based on state control of finances and ownership of the means of production. To this extent, the new regime created by the October Revolution of 1917 was a workers' state. But there was another side. Given the low level of the productive forces and the conditions of "generalized want" that persisted in Soviet Russia, the new state presided over a bourgeois—i.e., unequal—mode of distribution. This basic contradiction between the socialist form of property ownership and the bourgeois form of distribution imparted to the Soviet regime its peculiar and increasingly repressive form.

43.   Trotsky and his supporters—including many of the most important leaders of the Russian Revolution—formed the Left Opposition in 1923 to reform Communist Party policy in the Soviet Union and fight for a correct line in the Communist International. Supporters of the Left Opposition criticized the decay in inner-party democracy and advocated an economic policy that placed greater emphasis on the development of state industry, to strengthen socialist planning and bring down the prices of industrial goods. The Stalin faction pushed for greater market liberalization, an orientation to better-off sections of the peasantry (the kulaks), and limited development of the state sector and economic planning. The death of Lenin in January 1924 strengthened the faction led by Stalin. In his last writings, Lenin had warned of the increasing bureaucratization of the Communist Party and called for the removal of Stalin as general secretary.

The Consequences of "Socialism in One Country"

44.   While Trotsky and the Left Opposition fought for the implementation of a correct economic policy within the Soviet Union, they insisted that the fate of the revolutionary regime depended on the extension

of the revolution beyond the borders of the USSR. Without the victory of the working class in the advanced capitalist countries of Europe and North America, the Soviet state would not survive. It was on this very question that the conflict between the Left Opposition and the Stalinist bureaucracy centered. In 1924 Stalin, with the support of Bukharin, proposed that socialism could be built on a nationalist basis in the USSR. The promulgation of the theory of "socialism in one country" represented a fundamental repudiation of an essential tenet of Marxist theory and the world revolutionary perspective upon which the October Revolution had been based. It marked a turning point in the history of the USSR: the policies of the Soviet Union were severed by the bureaucracy from the fate of the world socialist revolution. The material interests that found expression in the program of "national socialism" were those of the bureaucracy itself. To the extent that state property was the source of its income and privileges, a nationalist policy of an essentially defensive character served the interests of the Stalinist regime. In the sphere of foreign policy, opportunist calculations of "national interest" replaced principled internationalist revolutionary considerations. The Stalinist regime converted the Communist International into an instrument of a nationalist Soviet foreign policy, utilizing local Communist parties to exert pressure on bourgeois governments. Herein lay the political origins of the class collaborationist policies that would eventually transform the Stalinist parties into instruments of political counterrevolution.

45.   The international consequences of the shift in Soviet policy were demonstrated in the defeat of the general strike in Britain in May 1926. Stalin, seeking to curry favor with the national leadership of the British trade unions, instructed the British Communist Party to give the General Council of the Trades Union Congress (TUC), controlled by the bureaucracy, uncritical support in the build-up to, and during, the general strike. This left the working class unprepared for the TUC's betrayal of the strike.

46.   Even greater disasters followed. The Soviet bureaucracy attacked the Theory of Permanent Revolution and revived the Menshevik two-stage theory of revolution in countries with a belated capitalist development. In China in 1925-1927, Stalin directed the Communist Party to support the national bourgeois movement of the Kuomintang on the basis of the theory of the "Bloc of Four Classes" against imperialism. Trotsky vehemently

opposed this class-collaborationist policy and warned of its devastating consequences for the socialist revolution in China. The fact that China was oppressed by imperialism did not lessen the conflict between the Chinese bourgeoisie and the working class. Indeed, the opposite was the case. As Trotsky wrote:

> The powerful role of foreign capital in the life of China has caused very strong sections of the Chinese bourgeoisie, the bureaucracy, and the military to join their destiny with that of imperialism. Without this tie, the enormous role of the so-called militarists in the life of modern China would be inconceivable.
>
> It would further be profound naiveté to believe that an abyss lies between the so-called comprador bourgeoisie, that is, the economic and political agency of foreign capital in China, and the so-called national bourgeoisie. No, these two sections stand incomparably closer to each other than the bourgeoisie and the masses of workers and peasants...
>
> It is a gross mistake to think that imperialism mechanically welds together all the classes of China from without... The revolutionary struggle against imperialism does not weaken, but rather strengthens the political differentiation of the classes.[30]

47.   Trotsky's warnings were confirmed. In April 1927 the military forces of the Kuomintang, under the leadership of Chiang Kai-shek, carried out a massacre of the Shanghai working class. A large section of the Chinese Communist Party leadership was murdered by the bourgeois nationalist forces. After April 1927, the Chinese Communist Party was ordered to enter the "left" Kuomintang led by Wang Ching-wei. The "left" Wang Ching-wei crushed the workers' and peasants' movement no less brutally than Chiang Kai-shek. Then, in August 1927, after the nearly complete demoralization of the Communist Party, the leadership of the Comintern demanded an immediate transition to armed insurrection. An attempt to implement this policy in Canton was drowned in blood

---

30 "The Chinese Revolution and the Theses of Comrade Stalin," in: *Leon Trotsky on China* (New York: Pathfinder, 1976), pp. 176-77.

within just three days. These catastrophic defeats, which were to have such a far-reaching impact on the history of the 20th century, effectively marked the end of the CCP as a mass party of the Chinese working class. Fleeing into the countryside to escape the consequences of the disaster produced by Stalin's policies, the surviving remnants of the CCP leadership, including Mao Zedong, reestablished the Communist Party as a peasant-based organization. It is not possible to understand the subsequent history of China—including its present-day emergence as a bastion of the most rapacious forms of capitalist exploitation—except within the context of Trotsky's critique of Stalin's "Bloc of Four Classes" and the tragedy of 1927.

The Expulsion of Trotsky

48.   The defeats in Britain and China diminished the revolutionary confidence of the Soviet working class. This, in turn, strengthened the bureaucracy and deepened its alienation from the working class. Power in the Soviet Union was consolidated in the hands of a bureaucratic clique headed by Stalin. In 1926, the Left Opposition briefly united with Kamenev and Zinoviev to form the United Opposition. In July-October 1926, Kamenev and Trotsky were expelled from the Politburo, and in November 1927 Trotsky and Zinoviev were expelled from the Russian Communist Party. In December, all supporters of the Left Opposition were expelled from the party. While Zinoviev and Kamenev subsequently capitulated to Stalin and rejoined the Communist Party, Trotsky was exiled to Alma Ata in January 1928, and was expelled from the Soviet Union in February 1929.

49.   From the beginning of his final exile, Trotsky insisted that all the differences between the Stalinist faction and the Left Opposition stemmed from their adherence to two irreconcilably opposed conceptions of socialism. The Stalinists proceeded from the possibility of constructing an isolated national socialist society, based on the resources of Russia; the Left Opposition insisted that the fate of the workers' state and its progress toward socialism was inextricably linked to the development of world socialist revolution. In his 1930 preface to a German edition of a pamphlet

that he had written two years earlier, entitled *The Permanent Revolution*, Trotsky summed up the essential issue:

> Marxism takes its point of departure from world economy, not as a sum of national parts but as a mighty and independent reality which has been created by the international division of labor and the world market, and which in our epoch imperiously dominates the national markets. The productive forces of capitalist society have long ago outgrown the national boundaries. The imperialist war (of 1914-1918) was one of the expressions of this fact. In respect of the technique of production, socialist society must represent a stage higher than capitalism. To aim at building a nationally isolated socialist society means, in spite of all passing successes, to pull the productive forces backward, even as compared with capitalism. To attempt, regardless of the geographical, cultural and historical conditions of the country's development, which constitutes a part of the world unity, to realize a shut-off proportionality of all the branches of economy within a national framework, means to pursue a reactionary utopia.[31]

50.   The political implications of Trotsky's critique of Stalin's national socialist perspective extended beyond the problems of Soviet policy. At stake were fundamental questions of the global perspective and strategic tasks of the international working class in the imperialist epoch. Trotsky wrote:

> The completion of the socialist revolution within national limits is unthinkable. One of the basic reasons for the crisis in bourgeois society is the fact that the productive forces created by it can no longer be reconciled with the framework of the national state. From this follow, on the one hand, imperialist wars, on the other, the utopia of a bourgeois United States of Europe. The socialist revolution begins on the national arena, it unfolds on the international arena, and is completed on the world arena. Thus, the socialist revolution

---

31   Leon Trotsky, *The Permanent Revolution* (London: New Park Publications, 1971), p. 22.

becomes a permanent revolution in a newer and broader sense of the word; it attains completion only in the final victory of the new society on our entire planet.[32]

The Early Struggles of the International Left Opposition

51. The Left Opposition found support outside the Russian Communist Party. A breakthrough occurred when Trotsky's *Critique of the Draft Program of the Comintern*, prepared for the Sixth Congress held in 1928, fell, through a stroke of luck, into the hands of James P. Cannon, a veteran revolutionary and founding member of the American Communist Party. After studying the document, he and the Canadian revolutionary, Maurice Spector, decided to take up the fight for Trotsky's positions. Soon after returning to the United States, Cannon—supported by Max Shachtman and Martin Abern—initiated the struggle for the positions of the Left Opposition within the Communist Party. A statement written by Cannon, Shachtman and Abern was presented to a meeting of the Political Committee of the Communist Party on October 27, 1928. It declared:

> The attempts to revise the basic Marxist-Leninist doctrine with the spurious theory of socialism in one country have been rightly resisted by the Opposition led by Trotsky. A number of revisionist and opportunist errors in various fields of Comintern activity and its ideological life in general have proceeded from this false theory. To this, in part at least, can be traced the false line in the Chinese revolution, the debacle of the Anglo-Russian Committee, the alarming and unprecedented growth of bureaucratism in the Comintern, an incorrect attitude and policy in the Soviet Union, etc., etc. This new "theory" is bound up with an overemphasis on the power and duration of the temporary stabilization of capitalism. Herein lies the true source of pessimism regarding the development of the proletarian world revolution. One of the principal duties of every Communist in every party of the Comintern is to fight along with

32 Ibid., p. 155.

the Opposition for the teachings of Marx, Engels and Lenin on this basic question.[33]

52.   Cannon was expelled at that very session of the Political Committee. He proceeded to found the Communist League of America. Thus, the Trotskyist movement in the United States, which was to play such a significant role in the development of the international Trotskyist movement, began on a principled foundation. Its point of departure was not a dispute over organizational issues or national tactics, but, rather, the decisive questions of international revolutionary strategy. The document that inspired Cannon, Trotsky's *Critique of the Draft Program*, was a comprehensive indictment of the nationalist orientation of the Stalin leadership and its failure to assess the strategic experiences of the international working class since the October Revolution of 1917. In his assessment of the world political and economic situation, Trotsky criticized the draft program's failure to analyze the rise of American imperialism and called attention to the implications of the struggle of American imperialism to establish and maintain its hegemonic position. While foreseeing a major economic crisis in the United States, he did not believe that this would lessen America's dominant position in world politics:

> Just the contrary is the case. In the period of crisis the hegemony of the United States will operate more completely, more openly, and more ruthlessly than in the period of boom. The United States will seek to overcome and extricate herself from her difficulties and maladies at the expense of Europe, regardless of whether this occurs in Asia, Canada, South America, Australia, or Europe itself, or whether this takes place peacefully or through war.[34]

53.   The Wall Street crash of October 1929 marked the beginning of a global depression that plunged capitalism into the greatest crisis in its

---

33   James P. Cannon, *The Left Opposition in the United States 1928-31* (New York: Monad Press, 1981), p. 32.

34   Leon Trotsky, *The Third International After Lenin* (New York: Pathfinder, 2002), pp. 28-29.

history. Beginning little more than a decade after the end of World War I, the Great Depression of the 1930s, and the bloody social and political upheavals that arose out of it, provided another crushing refutation of all the complacent nostrums of the revisionists and reformists. Capitalism was brought by its own contradictions to the brink of collapse in Europe, Asia and even North America. That it survived these upheavals, at an incredible cost in human lives, is attributable to the political betrayals of the mass organizations of the working class led, first and foremost, by the Stalinists and Social Democrats. The Fourth International arose on the basis of the struggle, led by Trotsky, against these betrayals. The record and lessons of these struggles form, to this day, the essential historical, theoretical and political foundation for the education of Marxists.

54.   After his arrival in Turkey in 1929, Trotsky continued to fight for a correct policy in the Soviet Union, calling for a planned and rational program of industrialization. The aim of the International Left Opposition remained the political reform of the regime in the Soviet Union, and the return of the Communist International to a correct revolutionary line, based on Marxist principles. In the late 1920s, in the face of mass famine caused by the peasantry's withholding of grain from the cities, the Stalinist bureaucracy reversed its previous orientation to the peasantry and promotion of market policies with a brutal and unplanned program of industrialization, collectivization of agriculture, and the "liquidation of the kulaks as a class." Its program of rapid industrialization, based on the perspective of economic nationalism and autarky, bore no relation to Trotsky's proposals for a planned program of state industrial development that utilized the resources of the world economy and its international division of labor. Ultra-leftism in domestic policy was accompanied by a sharp turn in the Comintern to sectarian political adventurism, based on the theory of the "Third Period." The political perspective promoted by this "theory"—or, to be more precise, anti-theory—hypothesized a continuous "radicalization of the masses," devoid of contradictions and apparently unrelated to objective economic, political and social processes. All problems of political strategy and tactics were reduced by the Stalinists to the simplistic shouting of radical slogans. Trotsky warned that the Stalinist hypothesis made a mockery of Marxist political analysis. He wrote:

It goes without saying that from the point of view of our epoch as a whole the development of the proletariat advances in the direction of the revolution. But this is not a steady progression, any more than the objective process of the deepening of capitalist contradictions. The reformists see only the ups of the capitalist road. The formal "revolutionaries" see only its downs. But a Marxist sees the road as a whole, all of its conjunctural ups and downs, without for a moment losing sight of the main direction—the catastrophe of wars, the explosion of revolutions.[35]

The Victory of Fascism in Germany

55.   Under the influence of "Third Period" policy, the Communist Parties were instructed to replace their adaptation to the trade unions, Social-Democratic parties, and bourgeois nationalists with an ultra-left program that included the formation of independent "red" unions and the rejection of the tactic of the united front. The united front tactic was replaced with the designation of Social-Democratic parties as "social fascist."

56.   The new policy of the Comintern was to have disastrous consequences in Germany, where the rise of fascism posed a mortal challenge to the socialist movement. Fascism was a movement of the demoralized petty bourgeoisie, devastated by the economic crisis and squeezed between the two main classes, the bourgeoisie and the working class. The defeats of the socialist movement had convinced broad sections of the petty bourgeoisie that the working class was not the solution but the source of its problems. The German bourgeoisie employed the fascists to destroy the labor organizations and atomize the working class. The victory of Hitler's Nazi Party in January 1933 was the result of the betrayals of Social Democracy and Stalinism. The Social Democrats placed their confidence in the bourgeois Weimar Republic and tied the working class to the capitalist state. The Stalinist policy of "social fascism"—which claimed that the SPD and

---

35   "The 'Third Period' of the Comintern's Errors," in: *Writings of Leon Trotsky 1930* (New York: Pathfinder Press, 1975), p. 28.

Hitler's party were "twins"—opposed all forms of collaboration between the Communist Party and the Social Democracy, even for defensive purposes. It deprived the Communist Party of any means of winning the confidence of workers still loyal to the SPD. As the Communist Party leadership developed the criminally complacent slogan, "After Hitler, us," Trotsky warned in December 1931, "Worker-Communists, you are hundreds of thousands, millions; you cannot leave for any place; there are not enough passports for you. Should fascism come to power, it will ride over your skulls and spines like a terrific tank. Your salvation lies in merciless struggle. And only a fighting unity with the Social Democratic workers can bring victory. Make haste, worker-Communists, you have very little time left!"[36] This warning was tragically confirmed after Hitler came to power in 1933 and proceeded to arrest or execute the leadership of the working class and destroy its independent organizations.

57.   The victory of fascism in Germany was a turning point in the degeneration of the Communist Parties. Despite the unprecedented magnitude of the defeat suffered in Germany, there was no opposition within the parties of the Communist International. In response, Trotsky issued the call for the founding of new parties and a new International. "The Moscow leadership has not only proclaimed as infallible the policy which guaranteed victory to Hitler, but has also prohibited all discussion of what had occurred," he wrote in July 1933. "And this shameful interdiction was not violated, nor overthrown. No national congresses; no international congress; no discussions at party meetings; no discussion in the press! An organization which was not roused by the thunder of fascism and which submits docilely to such outrageous acts of the bureaucracy demonstrates thereby that it is dead and that nothing can ever revive it."[37] While Trotsky continued to define the Soviet Union as a workers' state, albeit one that had undergone a far-reaching degeneration, he warned that its long-term survival, not to mention its development along genuinely socialist lines, depended upon the overthrow of the bureaucracy in a political revolution.

---

36 "For a Workers' United Front Against Fascism" in *The Struggle Against Fascism in Germany* (New York: Pathfinder Press, 1971) p. 141.

37 "It is Necessary to Build Communist Parties and an International Anew" in *The Struggle Against Fascism in Germany*, p. 420.

The Fourth International and the Struggle against Centrism

58.   The call for the Fourth International was not a tactical maneuver. It was based on an assessment of the social and political transformation of the Soviet regime, the Communist International and their relationship to the working class. On this point Trotsky came into conflict during the mid-1930s with political tendencies that he defined as "centrist." While proclaiming their devotion to socialist revolution, these groups opposed the formation of the Fourth International. They sought, rather, to find some sort of middle ground between Stalinism and Trotskyism, and between reformist and revolutionary policies.

59.   Trotsky wrote in 1934 that a centrist "views with hatred the revolutionary principle: state what is. He is inclined to substitute for a principled policy personal maneuvering and petty organizational diplomacy." Trotsky explained, "A centrist occupies a position between an opportunist and a Marxist somewhat analogous to that which a petty bourgeois occupies between a capitalist and a proletarian: he kowtows before the first and has contempt for the second." Another feature of centrism was that it did not "understand that in the present epoch a national revolutionary party can be built only as part of an international party. In his choice of his international allies, the centrist is even less discriminating than in his own country."[38]

60.   As the working class moved to the left in response to the menace of fascism, the centrist groups blocked the formation of a genuinely revolutionary party. The centrist tendencies—including the Independent Labor Party in Britain, the German-émigré SAP (in which Willy Brandt, the future SPD leader and German Chancellor, played a leading and treacherous role), the Spanish POUM, and others—attempted to find a halfway house between revolutionary and reformist politics. Underlying their claims that it would be "premature" to proclaim the founding of the Fourth International was (1) a basic disagreement with Trotsky's characterization of the Stalinist regime and its affiliated parties as counterrevolutionary, and (2) a refusal to break with the opportunist political relations that prevailed within their national milieu.

---

38 "Centrism and the Fourth International," in: *Writings of Leon Trotsky 1933-34* (New York: Pathfinder, 1998), p. 233.

The Treachery of the Popular Front

61.   The evasions and vacillations of the centrist tendencies under-mined the struggle against Stalinism under conditions in which the poli-cies of the Soviet regime had assumed an openly counter-revolutionary character. Having opposed Trotsky's call for a "united front" of working class parties against Hitler in Germany, the Stalinists swung in the other direction after the victory of the Nazis. At the Seventh Congress of the Comintern in 1935, they unveiled a new program—the "Popular Front." This called for, in the name of the struggle against fascism and the de-fense of democracy, the formation of political alliances with "democratic" bourgeois parties. The practical effect of these alliances was the political subordination of the working class to the bourgeoisie, private property and the capitalist state. While politically catastrophic for the working class, the Popular Front served the interests of the Soviet bureaucracy. By offering to use the local Communist parties as instruments for the suppression of rev-olutionary struggle by the working class, Stalin hoped to curry favor with bourgeois regimes and improve the diplomatic position of the USSR. In fact, whatever the limited and short-term diplomatic gains achieved on the basis of this strategy, the defeats of the working class produced by "Popular Frontism" profoundly weakened the Soviet Union.

62.   Stalinist policy was consciously directed against the revolutionary seizure of power by the working class. Stalin feared that the victory of the working class, especially in Western Europe, would rekindle the revolu-tionary movement of the Soviet working class. In 1936-38, the Stalinists helped strangle a revolutionary situation in France, which was touched off by a general strike in June 1936. The Popular Front regime supported by the French Communist Party demoralized the working class and cleared the path for the capitulation of the French bourgeoisie to Hitler in June 1940. In the Spanish Revolution, the Stalinists supported the bourgeois government of Azaña. The Spanish Communist Party became the prin-cipal prop of capitalist property and bourgeois law and order. It recruited heavily among better-off sections of the urban middle class who desper-ately feared socialist revolution. Stalin flooded Spain with GPU agents who carried out a reign of terror against revolutionary socialist tendencies. His agents organized the suppression of the working class insurrection

in Barcelona, and they kidnapped, tortured and murdered Andres Nin, leader of the POUM. The Stalinists' liquidation of the POUM was facilitated, tragically, by the centrist policies pursued by Nin, who had entered into the popular front government in Barcelona. In the United States, the Communist Party supported the Democratic Party and the administration of Franklin Delano Roosevelt.

63. The purpose of Popular Frontism—which Trotsky defined as the alliance of bourgeois liberalism with the GPU—was the defense of capitalist property against the menace of socialist revolution. The rhetorical tributes to "democracy" were employed to facilitate the political disarming of the working class as an independent force, while concealing the class interests served by the "democratic" state. To the extent that the working class was prevented from fighting for political power, the struggle against the real threats to democracy was fatally handicapped. As demonstrated in France and Spain, the attempt to defend democracy without fighting for socialism proved bankrupt and ended in disaster. Among the arguments repeatedly made by the Stalinists in both Spain and France was that revolutionary policies "frightened" the petty bourgeoisie and turned them in the direction of the fascists. Thus, the working class could retain the sympathy of the middle class only by eschewing socialist demands that threatened private property and by giving support to moderate bourgeois leaders within the framework of the Popular Front. Trotsky emphatically rejected this cowardly and defeatist approach, which expressed a total misappraisal of the social psychology of the middle classes:

> It is false, thrice false, to affirm that the present petty bourgeoisie is not going to the working class parties because it fears "extreme measures." Quite the contrary. The lower petty bourgeoisie, in its great masses, only sees in the working class parties parliamentary machines. They do not believe in their strength, nor in their capacity to struggle, in their readiness this time to conduct the struggle to the end.
>
> And if this is so, is it worth the trouble to replace Radicalism [the "left" bourgeois political tendency] by its parliamentary colleagues on the Left? That is how the semi-expropriated, ruined and discontented proprietor reasons or feels. Without an understanding of this

psychology of the peasants, the artisans, the employees, the petty functionaries, etc.—a psychology that flows from the social crisis— it is impossible to elaborate a correct policy. The petty bourgeoisie is economically dependent and politically atomized. That is why it cannot conduct an independent policy. It needs a "leader" who inspires it with confidence. This individual or collective leadership, i.e., a personage or party, can be given to it by one or the other of the fundamental classes—either the big bourgeoisie or the proletariat. Fascism unites and arms the scattered masses. Out of human dust it organizes combat detachments. It thus gives the petty bourgeoisie the illusion of being an independent force. It begins to imagine that it will really command the state. It is not surprising that these illusions and hopes turn the head of the petty bourgeoisie!

But the petty bourgeoisie can also find a leader in the proletariat.[39]

64.   The transformation of the Comintern into an instrument of the Soviet bureaucracy was accompanied by a series of purges and expulsions, in which any leaders representing the traditions of revolutionary internationalism were replaced with loyal representatives of the apparatus. This transformation had begun in 1923 and continued throughout the 1930s, often as part of the struggle against Trotskyism. By the period of the "Popular Front," the Comintern had completely rejected the program of world revolution, to which Stalin referred as a "tragi-comic misunderstanding." The Comintern was finally dissolved in 1943, as a gesture to the Stalinist bureaucracy's imperialist allies.

The Revolution Betrayed

65.   In 1936 Trotsky wrote *The Revolution Betrayed*, which established the socio-economic necessity that motivated the fight for the Fourth International. In this monumental work, Trotsky uncovered the laws governing the emergence, growth and inevitable destruction of the Soviet bu-

---

39 Leon Trotsky, *Whither France* (London: New Park Publications, 1974), p. 13.

reaucracy, to which he refused to attribute any progressive historical role. Analyzing the contradictions that governed the existence of the bureaucracy as a privileged caste within a workers' state, Trotsky established that the conquests of the 1917 October Revolution could be preserved and extended only through the political revolution, in which the Soviet workers overthrew the bureaucracy through a violent insurrection, while preserving and developing the nationalized property relations established by the Bolshevik revolution. He defined the Soviet regime as transitional, whose fate depended upon the world revolution. Trotsky wrote:

> The USSR is a contradictory society halfway between capitalism and socialism, in which: (a) the productive forces are still far from adequate to give the state property a socialist character; (b) the tendency toward primitive accumulation created by want breaks out through innumerable pores of the planned economy; (c) norms of distribution preserving a bourgeois character lie at the basis of a new differentiation of society; (d) the economic growth, while slowly bettering the situation of the toilers, promotes the swift formation of a privileged stratum; (e) exploiting the social antagonisms, the bureaucracy has converted itself into an uncontrolled caste alien to socialism; (f) the social revolution, betrayed by the ruling party, still exists in property relations and in the consciousness of the toiling masses; (g) a further development of the accumulated contradictions can as well lead to socialism as back to capitalism; (h) on the road to capitalism the counterrevolution would have to break the resistance of the workers; (i) on the road to socialism the workers would have to overthrow the bureaucracy. In the last analysis, the question will be decided by a struggle of living social forces, both on the national and the world arena.[40]

66.   An objection to Trotsky's analysis of Soviet society, identified with the theory generally known as "state capitalism," is that the bureaucracy represented a new ruling class. Trotsky rejected this theory, which, in all its varia-

---

40 Leon Trotsky, *The Revolution Betrayed: What Is the Soviet Union and Where Is It Going?* (Detroit: Labor Publications, 1991), p. 216.

tions, fails to provide a Marxist substantiation of its characterization of the bureaucracy as a class. For Marxism, a class is distinguished by its independent roots in the economic structure of society. The existence of a class is bound up with historically specific forms of property and relations of production, which, in turn, are embodied in the activities of this social stratum. The Soviet bureaucracy did not represent such a historical force. It usurped political power; it administered the state; and it devoured a significant portion of the wealth of the Soviet Union. But the forms of property had emerged out of a working class revolution. Trotsky acknowledged that the overwhelming political control over the state exerted by the bureaucracy had created "a new and hitherto unknown relation between the bureaucracy and the riches of the nation."[41] He warned that this could lead, unless preempted by a political revolution, "to a complete liquidation of the social conquests of the proletarian revolution."[42] This is what eventually happened, some 55 years after the publication of *Revolution Betrayed*. However, the consequences of the dissolution of the USSR provided decisive confirmation of Trotsky's definition of the bureaucracy as a caste, rather than a class. The destruction of the USSR led rapidly to the liquidation of state property and its conversion into private property. Well-placed bureaucrats converted the state-owned industrial, financial and natural resources that they had previously administered into their personal assets. Inheritance laws were established which allowed this new bourgeoisie to pass its property, acquired almost entirely through the theft of state assets, to its spouses and children. A stock exchange was established. Labor was transformed into a commodity, regulated by the law of value. Whatever remained of state planning collapsed. Not a single special social attribute by which the ruling bureaucracy might have been legitimately identified as a distinct class survived the USSR. If what had existed prior to the dissolution of the Soviet Union was "state capitalism," it rapidly disappeared along with the workers' state! The "theory" of state capitalism contributed nothing to a sociological understanding of Soviet society, or to a political strategy for the revolutionary struggle against Stalinism.

67.   The Stalinist bureaucracy murdered virtually the entire leadership of the October Revolution. Show trials were organized, between 1936 and 1938,

---

41 Ibid., p. 211.

42 Ibid.

of Bolshevik leaders, including Zinoviev, Kamenev, Bukharin and Rakovsky. These gruesome proceedings, in which the defendants were compelled to denounce themselves (having been falsely promised that such confessions would save them and their families), ended invariably with the announcement of death sentences that were carried out within hours. In the few cases where prison sentences were imposed—as with Rakovsky and Radek—the defendants were later murdered in secret. The trials were the public image of an unprecedented campaign of mass murder conducted away from public view. Hundreds of thousands of socialists, the finest representatives of several political generations of Marxist intellectuals and workers, were physically exterminated. The fascist dictator Mussolini commented with admiration that Stalin's regime had killed far more communists than his own! Nearly one million people were killed in a wave of counter-revolutionary violence from 1936 to 1939. This liquidation—which confirmed, in the most direct sense, Trotsky's assessment of Stalin as the "gravedigger of the revolution"—dealt a blow to the revolutionary consciousness of the Soviet working class from which the Soviet Union never recovered. The history and record of these unparalleled crimes constitute the unanswerable refutation of the claim of countless bourgeois propagandists that Stalinism based itself on the theoretical and political heritage of Marxism, let alone the claim that Stalinism and Trotskyism were merely variants of one and the same Marxism. The real relationship between Stalinism and Trotskyism was described best by Trotsky: they were separated, he wrote, by "a river of blood."

The Founding of the Fourth International

68.   In September 1938, the Fourth International held its founding congress, a historical milestone for the socialist movement and the international working class. Its founding document, *The Death Agony of Capitalism and the Tasks of the Fourth International (The Mobilization of the Masses around Transitional Demands to Prepare the Conquest of Power)* was written by Trotsky and outlined the central tasks facing the socialist movement:

> Without a socialist revolution, in the next historical period at that, a catastrophe threatens the whole culture of mankind. The turn is

now to the proletariat, i.e., chiefly to its revolutionary vanguard. The historical crisis of mankind is reduced to the crisis of the revolutionary leadership.[43]

69.   The only way out of this crisis of leadership was through the building of sections of the Fourth International in every country. Against the skeptics and centrists who argued that it was premature to build a new International, that it would have to arise out of "great events," Trotsky replied:

> The Fourth International has already arisen out of great events: the greatest defeats of the proletariat in history. The cause of these defeats is to be found in the degeneration and perfidy of the old leadership. The class struggle does not tolerate an interruption. The Third International, following the Second, is dead for purposes of revolution. Long live the Fourth International!
>
> But has the time yet arrived to proclaim its creation?...the skeptics are not quieted down. The Fourth International, we answer, has no need of being 'proclaimed.' It exists and it fights. It is weak? Yes, its ranks are not numerous because it is still young. They are as yet chiefly cadres. But these cadres are pledges for the future. Outside of these cadres there does not exist a single revolutionary current on this planet really meriting the name.[44]

70.   The subsequent history of the 20th century would prove the correctness of the assessment of the Fourth International as the only genuinely revolutionary leadership. The strategic task of the period was to bridge the gap between the maturity of the objective revolutionary conditions and the immaturity of the proletariat and its vanguard. To meet this challenge, the Fourth International formulated a series of economic and political demands—such as the sliding scale of wages and hours; the nationalization of industry, banks, and agriculture; the arming of the proletariat; the formation of a workers' and farmers' government—as a means

---

43 *The Death Agony of Capitalism and the Tasks of the Fourth International* (New York: Labor Publications, 1981), p. 2.

44 Ibid., p. 42.

of developing the revolutionary consciousness of the working class and exposing its old leaderships. The demands, Trotsky wrote, would constitute a bridge "stemming from today's conditions and from today's consciousness of wide layers of the working class and unalterably leading to one final conclusion, the conquest of power by the proletariat."[45] In later years, revisionist tendencies would seek to transform the *Transitional Program* into a recipe book for opportunist adaptation, by tearing isolated demands out of their revolutionary context and using them as a substitute for the struggle to win the working class to a socialist perspective and program. In this way, they sought to use fragments from the Transitional Program as a means of adapting to, rather than combating, the backward consciousness of the working class and the old reformist and Stalinist leaderships.

71.   In discussions held by Trotsky with leaders of the American Trotskyist movement in May 1938, he insisted that the program of the revolutionary party had to take as its point of departure the objective development of the crisis of world capitalism, not the subjective mood and existing level of working class consciousness. "The program," he insisted, "must express the objective tasks of the working class rather than the backwardness of the workers. It must reflect society as it is, and not the backwardness of the working class. It is an instrument to vanquish the backwardness. That is why we must express in our program the whole acuteness of the social crisis of the capitalist society, including in the first line the United States. We cannot postpone or modify objective conditions which don't depend upon us. We cannot guarantee that the masses will solve the crisis; but we must express the situation as it is, and that is the task of the program."[46]

The Outbreak of World War II and Trotsky's Last Struggle

72.   The signing of the Stalin-Hitler Pact in August 1939 and the subsequent outbreak of World War II led to a political crisis inside the

---

45 Ibid., p. 4.

46 *The Transitional Program for Socialist Revolution* (New York: Pathfinder, 2001), pp. 189-90.

Socialist Workers Party in the United States.[47] A political faction led
by Max Shachtman, James Burnham and Martin Abern argued that the
Soviet Union could no longer be designated a workers' state. Flowing from
this change in their definition of the class nature of the Soviet State—
which Burnham now characterized as "bureaucratic collectivist"—they
stated that the Fourth International should not call for the defense of the
USSR in the event of war.

73.   Trotsky replied that the characterization of the Stalinist regime as
"bureaucratic collectivist"—a new and unprecedented form of exploitative
society, unforeseen by Marxism—had far-reaching political and historical implications. At issue, in the final analysis, was the historical viability of
the Marxist project itself. The premise that underlay the Burnham thesis
(adopted somewhat later by Shachtman) was that the working class had
exhausted its potential as a revolutionary social force. The development
of modern society was leading not in the direction of socialism, achieved
on the basis of an international working class revolution. Rather, a form of
"bureaucratic collectivism" was emerging, in which society was controlled
and directed by a managerial elite. If Burnham was correct, it followed that
Marxism understood incorrectly the processes of modern history; and had
been mistaken in attributing to the working class a revolutionary role. But
Burnham's revisionist perspective was less the product of a materialist analysis of the economic foundations and social dynamics of modern capitalist society, let alone of the Soviet Union, than it was a cry of despair. From the defeats of the 1920s and 1930s, Burnham and Shachtman had concluded that
the socialist revolution was impossible. Trotsky rejected this impressionistic
and pessimistic position. The Fourth International, he wrote, upheld the revolutionary perspective of Marxism, and explained that the defeats suffered
by the working class were the outcome of the political betrayals of its mass
organizations. In opposition to this analysis, wrote Trotsky:

> ...All the various types of disillusioned and frightened represen-
> tatives of pseudo-Marxism proceed on the contrary from the as-

---

47 The SWP was founded in January 1938, almost a decade after Cannon initiated the
fight for Trotskyism in the United States. During these 10 years, the American Trotskyists
established a significant presence in the struggles of the working class. Their leadership of
the Minneapolis General Strike in 1934 attracted national and worldwide attention.

sumption that the bankruptcy of the leadership only "reflects" the incapacity of the proletariat to fulfill its revolutionary mission. Not all our opponents express this thought clearly, but all of them—ultra-lefts, centrists, anarchists, not to mention Stalinists and social-democrats—shift the responsibility for the defeats from themselves to the shoulders of the proletariat. None of them indicate under precisely what conditions the proletariat will be capable of accomplishing the socialist overturn.[48]

74.   Trotsky insisted that the conflict within the SWP over program reflected two irreconcilably opposed conceptions of contemporary social processes:

> If we grant as true that the cause of the defeats is rooted in the social qualities of the proletariat itself then the position of modern society will have to be acknowledged as hopeless. ... Altogether differently does the case present itself to him who has clarified in his mind the profound antagonism between the organic, deep-going, insurmountable urge of the toiling masses to tear themselves free from the bloody capitalist chaos, and the conservative, patriotic, utterly bourgeois character of the outlived labor leadership. We must choose one of these two irreconcilable conceptions.[49]

75.   The Fourth International was to confront again and again, in diverse forms, political and theoretical tendencies that proceeded from the premise that the working class was not a revolutionary force. Whether in the form of Pabloism or other demoralized radical and "New Left" tendencies influenced by the theoreticians of the "Frankfurt School" (Marcuse, Adorno, Horkheimer, et al.), the rejection of the revolutionary role of the working class formed the basis of their opportunist political outlook. As for Shachtman and Burnham, their subsequent evolution vindicated Trotsky's analysis. In April 1940 Burnham and Shachtman split from the SWP and formed the "Workers Party." Within a month, Burnham resigned from his

---

48   Leon Trotsky, *In Defense of Marxism* (London: New Park, 1971), p. 15.

49   Ibid.

own creation and declared that he no longer considered himself a Marxist or a socialist. This marked the beginning of a rapid evolution to the extreme right. He became an advocate of preemptive nuclear war against the USSR, and, by the 1950s, the principal ideologist of the emerging neo-conservative movement. In 1982, several years before his death, Burnham was awarded the Medal of Freedom by President Ronald Reagan. Shachtman's movement to the right proceeded at a somewhat slower pace, but was no less fundamental. He became a political adviser to the anti-communist AFL-CIO bureaucracy and to the most reactionary Cold War wing of the Democratic Party. Before his death in 1972, Shachtman supported the bombing of North Vietnam by the United States.

Trotsky's Defense of Materialist Dialectics

76.   Another element of the 1939-40 struggle requires attention: its explicitly theoretical-philosophical dimension. Burnham, a professor of philosophy at New York University, declared himself an opponent of materialist dialectics. Like many others who opposed dialectical materialism from the standpoint of philosophical idealism (especially in its neo-Kantian form), Burnham dismissed the materialism defended by Marx and Engels as merely a product of outdated 19th century science and its excessive reverence for Darwin's evolutionary theory. As for dialectics, Burnham ridiculed Hegel as "the century-dead arch-muddler of human thought."[50] In his reply to Burnham, Trotsky provided a succinct characterization of both materialist dialectics and the professor's theoretical method, explaining the relationship between Burnham's pragmatic outlook and his political conclusions:

> Vulgar thought operates with such concepts as capitalism, morals, freedom, workers' state, etc. as fixed abstractions, presuming that capitalism is equal to capitalism; morals are equal to morals, etc. Dialectical thinking analyzes all things and phenomena in their continuous change, while determining in the material conditions of

---

50   Ibid., p. 236.

those changes that critical limit beyond which 'A' ceases to be 'A', a workers' state ceases to be a workers' state.

The fundamental flaw of vulgar thought lies in the fact that it wishes to content itself with motionless imprints of a reality which consists of eternal motion. Dialectical thinking gives to concepts, by means of closer approximations, corrections, concretization, a richness of content and flexibility; I would even say a succulence which to a certain extent brings them close to living phenomena. Not capitalism in general, but a given capitalism at a given stage of development. Not a workers' state in general, but a given workers' state in a backward country in an imperialist encirclement, etc.

Dialectical thinking is related to vulgar thinking in the same way that a motion picture is related to a still photograph. The motion picture does not outlaw the still photograph but combines a series of them according to the laws of motion. Dialectics does not deny the syllogism, but teaches us to combine syllogisms in such a way as to bring our understanding closer to the eternally changing reality. Hegel in his *Logic* established a series of laws: change of quantity into quality, development through contradictions, conflict of content and form, interruption of continuity, change of possibility into inevitability, etc., which are just as important for theoretical thought as is the simple syllogism for more elementary tasks.

Hegel wrote before Darwin and before Marx. Thanks to the powerful impulse given to thought by the French Revolution, Hegel anticipated the general movement of science. But because it was only an anticipation, although by a genius, it received from Hegel an idealistic character. Hegel operated with ideological shadows as the ultimate reality. Marx demonstrated that the movement of these ideological shadows reflected nothing but the movement of material bodies.

We call our dialectic, materialist, since its roots are neither in heaven nor in the depths of our 'free will,' but in objective reality, in nature. Consciousness grew out of the unconscious, psychology out of physiology, the organic world out of the inorganic, the solar system out of the nebulae. On all the rungs of the ladder of development, the quantitative changes were transformed into the qualitative. Our thought, including dialectical thought, is only one of the forms of the expression of changing matter. There is place within this system for neither God, nor Devil, nor immortal soul, nor eternal norms of laws and morals. The dialectic of thinking, having grown out of the dialectic of nature, possesses consequently a thoroughly materialist character.[51]

77.   Shachtman asserted that no one had demonstrated "that agreement or disagreement on the more abstract doctrines of dialectical materialism necessarily affects today's and tomorrow's concrete political issues— and political parties, programs and struggles are based on such concrete issues." Trotsky replied:

> ...What parties? What programs? What struggles? All parties and all programs are here lumped together. The party of the proletariat is a party unlike all the rest. It is not at all based upon "such concrete issues." In its very foundation it is diametrically opposed to the parties of the bourgeois horse-traders and petty-bourgeois rag patchers. Its task is the preparation of a social revolution and the regeneration of mankind on new material and moral foundations. In order not to give way under the pressure of bourgeois public opinion and police repression, the proletarian revolutionist, a leader all the more, requires a clear, far-sighted, completely thought-out world outlook. Only upon the basis of a unified Marxist conception is it possible to correctly approach 'concrete' questions.[52]

The Petty-Bourgeois Opposition and Party Organization

78.   At an early stage of the factional struggle inside the SWP, Trotsky defined the Shachtman-Burnham-Abern minority as "a typical petty-bourgeois tendency." This was not a gratuitous insult. Rather, on the basis of political experience spanning more than 40 years, and which included

51   Ibid., pp. 65-66.
52   Ibid., pp. 143-44.

leading two revolutions (in 1905 and 1917) and creating and commanding the Red Army, Trotsky detected in the minority features characteristic of "any petty-bourgeois group inside the socialist movement." The list included: "a disdainful attitude toward theory and an inclination toward eclecticism; disrespect for the tradition of their own organization; anxiety for personal 'independence' at the expense of anxiety for objective truth; nervousness instead of consistency; readiness to jump from one position to another; lack of understanding of revolutionary centralism and hostility towards it; and finally, inclination to substitute clique ties and personal relationships for party discipline."[53]

79.   The minority relentlessly denounced the organizational practices of the SWP, all-but-depicting Cannon as an emerging Stalin, the boss of a ruthless party bureaucracy dedicated to stamping out all expressions of individuality. Cannon, not one to mince words, remarked that

> The petty-bourgeois intellectuals are introspective by nature. They mistake their own emotions, their uncertainties, their fears and their own egoistic concern about their personal fate for the sentiments and movements of the great masses. They measure the world's agony by their own inconsequential aches and pains.[54]

80.   Cannon pointed out that the petty-bourgeois minority's denunciation of the party's organizational practices followed a familiar pattern:

> ...The history of the revolutionary labor movement since the days of the First International is an uninterrupted chronicle of the attempts of petty-bourgeois groupings and tendencies of all kinds to recompense themselves for their theoretical and political weakness by furious attacks against the "organizational methods" of the Marxists. And under the heading of organizational methods, they include everything from the concept of revolutionary centralism up to routine matters of administration; and beyond that to

---

53 Ibid., p. 56.

54 James P. Cannon, *The Struggle for a Proletarian Party* (New York: Pathfinder Press, 1977), p. 6.

the personal manners and methods of their principled opponents, which they invariably describe as "bad," "harsh," "tyrannical," and— of course, of course, of course—"bureaucratic." To this day any little group of anarchists will explain to you how the "authoritarian" Marx mistreated Bakunin.

The eleven year history of the Trotskyist movement in the United States is extremely rich in such experiences. The internal struggles and faction fights, in which the basic cadres of our movement were consolidated and educated, were, in part, always struggles against attempts to replace principled issues by organizational quarrels. The politically weak opponents resorted to this subterfuge every time.[55]

81.   Trotsky warmly endorsed Cannon's analysis of the "organization question" and his struggle for a "proletarian orientation" by the SWP. He wrote: "Jim's pamphlet is excellent: It is the writing of a genuine workers' leader. If the discussion had not produced more than this document, it would be justified."[56]

The Fourth International and the Outbreak of World War II

82.   The Second World War erupted in September 1939 with the invasion of Poland by Nazi Germany. Hitler's bloody assault was facilitated by the signing of a "Non-Aggression Pact" with the Stalinist regime only one week earlier. The immediate political and military impulse for the launching of the conflagration came from the strategic objectives of the Third Reich. However, at a more fundamental level, the war arose out of the economic and geo-political contradictions generated by the First World War and, beyond that, the historic obsolescence of the nation-state system and the general economic breakdown of world capitalism. Trotsky dismissed attempts to portray the war as a conflict between democracy and fascism. "The present war," he wrote, "which its participants started before they signed the treaty of Versailles, grew out of imperialist contradictions.

---

55   Ibid., pp. 10-11.

56   *In Defense of Marxism*, p. 206.

It was as inevitable as the crash of trains which are let loose one toward the other on the same track."[57] In *The Manifesto of the Fourth International on the Imperialist War*, written in May 1940, Trotsky placed responsibility for the global catastrophe on the imperialist bourgeoisie of all the major capitalist countries. The belated denunciations by France, Britain and the United States of Hitler's totalitarian regime reeked of cynicism. Trotsky wrote:

> The democratic governments, who in their day hailed Hitler as a crusader against Bolshevism, now make him out to be some kind of Satan unexpectedly loosed from the depths of hell, who violates the sanctity of treaties, boundary lines, rules, and regulations. If it were not for Hitler the capitalist world would blossom like a garden. What a miserable lie! This German epileptic with a calculating machine in his skull and unlimited power in his hands did not fall from the sky or come up out of hell: he is nothing but the personification of all the destructive forces of imperialism. ... Hitler, rocking the old colonial powers to their foundations, does nothing but give a more finished expression to the imperialist will to power. Through Hitler, world capitalism, driven to desperation by its own impasse, has begun to press a razor-sharp dagger into its own bowels.
>
> The butchers of the second imperialist war will not succeed in transforming Hitler into a scapegoat for their own sins.
>
> Before the judgment bar of the proletariat all the present rulers will answer. Hitler will do no more than occupy first place among the criminals in the dock.[58]

83.   The *Manifesto* drew attention to the role of the United States. At the time (in 1940), it remained outside the direct sphere of conflict. But, Trotsky predicted, the American bourgeoisie would soon exploit the opportunity offered by war to secure for the United States a hegemonic

---

57 "Who is Guilty of Starting the Second World War?" in: *Writings of Leon Trotsky 1939-40* (New York: Pathfinder, 2001), p. 99.

58 "Manifesto of the Fourth International on the Imperialist War and the Proletarian World Revolution," in: *Writings of Leon Trotsky 1939-40* (New York: Pathfinder, 2001), p. 233.

position in the affairs of world capitalism. This was not simply a matter of ambition, but of economic and political necessity:

> The industrial, financial, and military strength of the United States, the foremost capitalist power in the world, does not at all insure the blossoming of American economic life, but on the contrary, invests the crisis of her social system with an especially malignant and convulsive character. Gold in the billions cannot be made use of, nor can the millions of unemployed! In the theses of the Fourth International, *War and the Fourth International*, published six years ago, it was predicted:
>
> "US capitalism is up against the same problems that pushed Germany in 1914 on the path of war. The world is divided? It must be redivided. For Germany it was a question of 'organizing Europe.' The United States must 'organize' the world. History is bringing humanity face to face with the volcanic eruption of American imperialism."[59]

84.   The *Manifesto* analyzed the driving forces guiding American imperialism:

> Under one or another pretext and slogan the United States will intervene in the tremendous clash in order to maintain its world dominion. The order and the time of the struggle between American capitalism and its enemies is not yet known—perhaps even by Washington. War with Japan would be a struggle for 'living room' in the Pacific Ocean. War in the Atlantic, even if directed immediately against Germany, would be a struggle for the heritage of Great Britain.
>
> The potential victory of Germany over the Allies hangs like a nightmare over Washington. With the European continent and the resources of its colonies as her base, with all the European munitions factories and shipyards at her disposal, Germany—especially in combination with Japan in the Orient—would constitute a mor-

---

59   Ibid., p. 227.

tal danger for American imperialism. The present titanic battles on the fields of Europe are, in this sense, preparatory episodes in the struggle between Germany and America.[60]

85.   The *Manifesto of the Fourth International* called on workers in the United States to oppose war, but explicitly denounced the pacifism of layers of the petty bourgeoisie:

> Our struggle against United States intervention into the war has nothing in common with isolationism and pacifism. We tell the workers openly that the imperialist government cannot fail to drag this country into war. The dispute within the ruling class involves only the question of when to enter the war and against whom to level the fire first. To count upon holding the United States to neutrality by means of newspaper articles and pacifist resolutions is like trying to hold back the tide with a broom. The real struggle against war means the class struggle against imperialism and a merciless exposure of petty-bourgeois pacifism. Only revolution could prevent the American bourgeoisie from intervening in the second imperialist war or beginning the third imperialist war. All other methods are either charlatanism or stupidity or a combination of both.[61]

86.   In opposition to petty bourgeois pacifists who counseled individual passive resistance to the war, the Fourth International called for the training of workers in military arts, but under the control of the trade unions and with working class officers. Within the United States and among its allies, the ruling class sought to sell the war by presenting it as a "war for democracy," exploiting the hatred felt by broad sections of the working class for the Nazi regime. After the German invasion of the Soviet Union in 1941, this slogan would be taken up by the Stalinists as part of their alliance with the Allied imperialist powers. The Fourth International rejected it from the outset:

---

60   Ibid.

61   Ibid., p. 229

No less a lie is the slogan of a war for democracy against fascism. As if the workers have forgotten that the British government helped Hitler and his hangman's crew gain power! The imperialist democracies are in reality the greatest aristocracies in history. England, France, Holland, Belgium rest on the enslavement of colonial peoples. The democracy of the United States rests upon the seizure of the vast wealth of an entire continent. All the efforts of these "democracies" are directed toward the preservation of their privileged position. A considerable portion of the war burden is unloaded by imperialist democracies onto their colonies. The slaves are obliged to furnish blood and gold in order to insure the possibility of their masters remaining slaveholders.[62]

87.   Trotsky insisted that the Stalin regime's initial wartime alliance with Germany, and its brutal policy in occupied Finland and Poland, did not alter the social character the Soviet Union as a degenerated workers' state. Despite the crimes and treachery of Stalinism, the Fourth International still called for the defense of the USSR against imperialism.

Many petty bourgeois radicals, who only yesterday were still ready to consider the Soviet Union as an axis for grouping the "democratic" forces against fascism, have suddenly discovered, now that their own fatherlands have been threatened by Hitler, that Moscow, which did not come to their aid, follows an imperialist policy, and that there is no difference between the USSR and the fascist countries.

"Lie!" will respond every class conscious worker—there is a difference. The bourgeoisie appraises this social difference better and more profoundly than do the radical windbags. To be sure, the nationalization of the means of production in one country, and a backward one at that, still does not insure the building of socialism. But it is capable of furthering the primary prerequisite of socialism, namely, the planned development of the productive forces. To turn one's back on the nationalization of the means of production on the

---

ground that in and of itself it does not create the well-being of the masses is tantamount to sentencing a granite foundation to destruction on the ground that it is impossible to live without walls and a roof.

88.   Defense of the Soviet Union from imperialism, however, did not in the least imply any political concession to the Stalinist bureaucracy:

> The Fourth International can defend the USSR only by the methods of revolutionary class struggle. To teach the workers correctly to understand the class character of the state—imperialist, colonial, workers'—and the reciprocal relations between them, as well as the inner contradictions in each of them, enables the workers to draw correct practical conclusions in every given situation. While waging a tireless struggle against the Moscow oligarchy, the Fourth International decisively rejects any policy that would aid imperialism against the USSR.
>
> The defense of the USSR coincides in principle with the preparation of the world proletarian revolution. We flatly reject the theory of socialism in one country, that brain child of ignorant and reactionary Stalinism. Only the world revolution can save the USSR for socialism. But the world revolution carries with it the inescapable blotting out of the Kremlin oligarchy.[63]

89.   The *Manifesto* concluded with the forceful reassertion of the Fourth International's strategy of world socialist revolution.

> In contradistinction to the Second and Third Internationals, the Fourth International builds its policy not on the military fortunes of the capitalist states but on the transformation of the imperialist war into a war of the workers against the capitalists, on the overthrow of the ruling classes of all countries, on the world socialist revolution. The shifts in the battle lines at the front, the destruction of national capitals, the occupation of territories, the downfall of individual

---

63   Ibid., pp. 239-40.

states, represent from this standpoint only tragic episodes on the road to the reconstruction of modern society.

Independently of the course of the war, we fulfill our basic task: we explain to the workers the irreconcilability between their interests and the interests of bloodthirsty capitalism; we mobilize the toilers against imperialism; we propagate the unity of the workers in all warring and neutral countries; we call for the fraternization of workers and soldiers within each country, and of soldiers with soldiers on the opposite side of the battle front; we mobilize the women and youth against the war; we carry on constant, persistent, tireless preparation for the revolution—in the factories, in the mills, in the villages, in the barracks, at the front, and in the fleet.[64]

Trotsky's Place In History

90.   The outbreak of war placed Trotsky's life in greater danger than ever. The revolutionary consequences of World War I remained fresh in the memory of the imperialist powers and the Soviet bureaucracy. As long as he lived, Trotsky remained the leader of the revolutionary government in exile. Was it not possible, even likely, Stalin feared, that the upheavals of war would create a revolutionary movement that would restore Trotsky to power? To complete the elimination of the leadership of the Russian Revolution and prevent the development of the Fourth International, Stalinist agents infiltrated the Trotskyist movement. Their central goal was the assassination of Leon Trotsky. Among those working for the GPU in the Trotskyist movement were Mark Zborowski (the secretary for Trotsky's son, Leon Sedov), Sylvia Callen (the secretary for James Cannon), and Joseph Hansen (Trotsky's secretary and guard after 1937 and future leader of the SWP). Zborowski, who was known as "Etienne" inside the Trotskyist movement, assisted the GPU in the assassinations of Erwin Wolf, one of Trotsky's secretaries, (in July 1937), Ignace Reiss, a defector from the GPU who had declared himself a Trotskyist, (in September 1937), Trotsky's son, Leon Sedov (in February 1938) and Rudolf Klement, secre-

---

64   Ibid., p. 265.

tary of the Fourth International (in July 1938, less than two months before the Fourth International's founding congress). On May 24, 1940, Trotsky escaped one attempt on his life, which had been facilitated by a GPU agent working on his guard detail (Robert Sheldon Harte). On August 20, 1940, Trotsky was assaulted by a GPU agent, Ramon Mercader, at his home in Coyoacan, Mexico. He died the next day.

91.   Trotsky's assassination was a devastating blow to the cause of international socialism. He was not only the co-leader of the October Revolution, the implacable opponent of Stalinism and the founder of the Fourth International. He was the last and greatest representative of the political, intellectual, cultural and moral traditions of the classical Marxism that had inspired the mass revolutionary workers' movement that emerged in the last decade of the 19th century and the first decades of the 20th. He developed a conception of revolutionary theory, rooted philosophically in materialism, directed outward toward the cognition of objective reality, oriented to the education and political mobilization of the working class, and strategically preoccupied with the revolutionary struggle against capitalism. Fully engaged in the historic tasks of the new revolutionary epoch, Trotsky viewed with contempt those who sought to evade their political responsibilities under the banner of personal freedom. "Let the philistines hunt for their own individuality in empty space," he declared. Nor did he give an inch to those who claimed that the defeats suffered by the working class demonstrated the failure of Marxism itself. For Trotsky, such arguments were based on political demoralization, not theoretical insight. Those shouting loudest about the "crisis of Marxism" were precisely those who had capitulated intellectually to the spread of political reaction. They were translating their personal fears, Trotsky wrote, "into the language of immaterial and universal criticism." The innumerable critics of Marxism, however, had no alternative but demoralized resignation for the working class. The opponents of Marxism, observed Trotsky, "are disarming themselves in the face of reaction, renouncing scientific social thought, surrendering not only material but also moral positions, and depriving themselves of any claim to revolutionary vengeance in the future."[65]

---

65   "Once Again on the 'Crisis of Marxism,'" in: *Writings of Leon Trotsky 1938-39* (New York: Pathfinder, 2002) pp. 238-39.

The United States Enters the War

92.   From the beginning of the war, the United States was engaged—politically, economically and even militarily—in the global conflict. The Roosevelt administration exploited the desperate situation confronting British Prime Minister, Winston Churchill, to extract political and financial concessions from British imperialism. In the long run, however, the United States could tolerate neither German dominance of Europe nor Japanese supremacy in Asia and the Pacific. In the latter case, the United States, since its bloody conquest of the Philippines at the turn of the 20th century, had come to regard the Pacific as an American lake, and China, since the crushing of the Boxer rebellion, as a US protectorate. Japan's attack on Pearl Harbor on December 7, 1941 provided Roosevelt the opportunity to realize the "rendezvous with destiny" that he had invoked just a few years earlier. The democratic pretensions used by American imperialism to justify its intervention were belied not only by the fact that millions of African Americans were deprived of their basic democratic rights throughout this period, but also by the anti-democratic measures employed during the war—including the internment of tens of thousands of Japanese and Japanese-Americans living in the United States. Much of the framework for the "national security state" was built up during the war years. Once the Soviet Union was attacked in June 1941 by Nazi Germany, the Stalinist parties became the most enthusiastic proponents of the "democratic" imperialist powers, shamelessly supporting a no-strike pledge in the United States.

93.   In the aftermath of Trotsky's assassination, the Socialist Workers Party upheld the perspective of proletarian internationalism and opposed the subordination of the working class to the imperialist war aims of the Roosevelt administration. For this reason, the SWP was the sole tendency in the workers' movement in the United States whose leaders were imprisoned during the war, and they were the first to be tried under the Smith Act of 1940 (which was later ruled unconstitutional). In 1941, 18 leaders and members of the SWP were framed-up and convicted of sedition. In line with its wartime alliance with American imperialism and its ruthless opposition to the Trotskyist movement, the Communist Party supported the trials. When CP members were prosecuted under the Smith Act fol-

lowing the war, the SWP took the principled position of defending them against attacks by the bourgeois state.

94.   The horrific events of World War II demonstrated the accuracy of Luxemburg's warning that the working class confronted only two options: socialism or barbarism. The crimes committed during the course of the war exposed before an entire generation the real face of capitalism. Six million Jews were killed in the Nazi Holocaust, along with some five million Roma, Soviet prisoners of war, Poles, and others targeted by the fascist regime. The United States government, which was indifferent to the Nazi program of mass extermination (refusing to bomb railroad tracks used to transport prisoners to their death) displayed its own barbaric potential through the dropping of two atomic bombs on civilian cities in Japan, killing between 200,000 and 350,000 people. The main purpose of this crime was to demonstrate to the world, and particularly the Soviet Union, the devastating potential of the new American weapon of mass destruction. In total, some 100 million people perished in six years of conflict. The war was the bitter price paid by the working class for the treachery of its leadership and the failure of the socialist revolution. The subsequent post-war boom was built upon this mountain of human corpses.

The End of the War and the "Buffer States"

95.   European capitalism was devastated economically by the war. Large sections of the bourgeoisie were discredited by their sponsorship of fascism. In this situation, the Soviet regime and its network of Stalinist parties played the decisive role in preventing the working class from taking power. The Stalinists utilized their political authority—which had been strengthened by the Soviet army's defeat of Hitler's forces—to divert the mass struggles that erupted in the closing stages and immediate aftermath of the war. In France, Italy, and Germany, the Kremlin instructed local Stalinist parties to support bourgeois governments, disarm resistance fighters, and suppress any independent initiative of the working class. Later, in Greece, the Soviet bureaucracy deprived insurgents of critical aid and guaranteed the victory of the bourgeoisie in the civil war.

96.   In Eastern Europe, where the Kremlin concluded that it could not tolerate, for reasons of military defense, the establishment of bourgeois puppet regimes controlled by the United States, the Soviet Union established a series of "buffer states" (East Germany, Poland, Hungary, Czechoslovakia, Bulgaria, and Romania) under its control. But the establishment of state property in these states (in some cases delayed for several years) was accompanied by the systematic disenfranchisement of the working class. The establishment of Stalinist-style police state regimes represented not the expansion of socialist revolution, but a peculiar and temporary arrangement that served, in the final analysis, the conservative aim of politically stabilizing post-war Europe. In Yugoslavia, nationalization took place in a somewhat different way than in the buffer states. Partisans, led by the Communist Party under Tito, came to power following the Second World War. While the legacy of the partisan war endowed Tito with a degree of legitimacy and popularity unknown in other Stalinist-controlled states, the working class was barred from creating its own Soviet-type institutions through which it could exercise political power. The Tito regime rapidly degenerated into a police-state, in which Tito himself played the role of arbiter between conflicting factions of a bureaucracy based on various national and ethnic constituencies. The unviable character of this set-up was exposed in the aftermath of Tito's death in 1980.

The United States and the Restabilization of Capitalism

97.   The betrayals of Stalinism gave the United States the necessary breathing space to consolidate its hegemony and begin to stabilize a shattered world economic system. A period of more sustained economic growth after the war was made possible on the basis of (1) the immense destruction of the European and Asian economies in the war, and (2) the economic strength of American industry based on advances in the productive process. American capitalism sought to "reorganize the world" through a financial and currency regime (the Bretton Woods System), within which the American dollar would play the role of world reserve currency, with fixed international exchange rates and dollar-gold convertibility. With the support of the other capitalist powers, it created institu-

tions such as the International Monetary Fund and the World Bank to regulate international economic affairs. With the Marshall Plan, begun in 1947, American capitalism sought to stimulate the economic recovery of Europe and Asia, which was the necessary foundation for the expansion of the US economy. On this basis of American hegemony over the capitalist system, world trade expanded rapidly following the war.

98. This international economic restabilization was the material foundation for national reformist policies in countries throughout the world. In the United States, the American bourgeoisie pursued a policy of Keynesian demand stimulation. It responded to the post-war strike wave by granting significant economic concessions to the industrial working class, continuing the reformist policies of the New Deal era that had been designed to avert social revolution. At the same time, with the support of the right-wing AFL and CIO trade union bureaucracies, it purged the trade unions and other American institutions of socialist-minded workers and members of the Communist Party. In Europe, a similar program of nationally-based social reform and labor-management collaboration was implemented with the active collaboration of the Social Democrats and trade unions. In the economically backward and former colonial countries, national bourgeois regimes were able to win a certain degree of independence, often by balancing between the Soviet Union and the United States. Through a policy that came to be known as import substitution industrialization, many former colonies were able to pursue a limited policy of domestic industrial development and agrarian reform. In the Soviet Union, the Stalinist bureaucracy oversaw a significant development of Soviet industry on the basis of national economic planning, albeit extremely distorted by the bureaucracy itself.

99. In international relations, the US sought to prevent any new eruption of direct conflict between the major capitalist powers, establishing institutions such as the United Nations to regulate international relations. The end of the war brought with it the beginning of the "Cold War" conflict between the United States and the Soviet Union. The immediate euphoria with which the American bourgeoisie greeted its nuclear monopoly was quickly shattered when the Soviet Union acquired the atomic bomb. A bitter struggle ensued within the political elite between those sections counseling the "containment" of the USSR and those advocating

its military "rollback." The logic of the latter position threatened to lead, as was well understood, to full-scale nuclear war. The conflict within the bourgeoisie came to a head in 1950, during the Korean War, when General Douglas MacArthur demanded that he be allowed to drop nuclear bombs on China to stop the advance of its troops into the Korean peninsula. Truman fired MacArthur. The "containment" faction had prevailed. For its part, the Stalinist bureaucracy set a strategic goal of accommodation with imperialism, expressed in the policy of "peaceful coexistence," a logical continuation of the theory of "socialism in one country." This uneasy truce, in which the two "superpowers" engaged in a nuclear arms race and competed for influence in the underdeveloped countries, frequently threatened to break out into full-scale conflict.

The Post-war Upsurge of the Masses

100.   Within the framework of the economic restabilization of world capitalism, the post-war period was characterized by an immense upsurge of the international working class and oppressed masses. In Asia, the Middle East, Africa and Latin America countless millions of workers and peasants sought to throw off the shackles of colonialism. These mass struggles imparted immense relevance to the Theory of Permanent Revolution and the lessons of Trotsky's struggle against Stalin's betrayal of the Chinese Revolution. Once again, the essential problems posed by the anti-imperialist struggle—the liquidation of the remnants of feudalism and the dominance of the latifundia; the end of colonial rule and the establishment of national independence; and the organization of economic life to end poverty and raise the social and cultural level of the masses—could be achieved only under the leadership of the revolutionary working class, armed with a genuinely democratic and international socialist program. But the objective necessity of such a program and perspective came up against the domination of the anti-imperialist movement by the national bourgeoisie, abetted by the Stalinist parties.

101.   In India, the Theory of Permanent Revolution was vindicated in the disastrous betrayal of the anti-imperialist independence movement by Gandhi, Nehru, and the bourgeois Congress Party in 1947-48. The

Indian bourgeoisie's acceptance of the country's partition into a predominantly Hindu India and Muslim Pakistan led immediately to communal conflict that cost up to one million lives. The dreadful legacy of partition is recorded in decades of war, violence and persistent mass poverty. In one form or another, the subordination of the working class to the bourgeois-led national movements produced political disaster in country after country. The key role was played by the Stalinist parties, which consistently advanced their class-collaborationist "two stage" theory of struggle—first independence under the leadership of the bourgeoisie and only later, at some unspecified point in the future, socialism—effectively blocking the struggle by the working class to establish its political hegemony in the mass anti-imperialist movement and take power.

102. In sharp contrast to the Stalinists, the Trotskyist movement in Ceylon (later Sri Lanka), organized in the Bolshevik-Leninist Party of India (BLPI), took a principled and internationalist position. It opposed the political settlement negotiated by the national bourgeoisie and British imperialism, which formally ended colonial status. This stand was vindicated almost immediately, when the bourgeoisie of Sri Lanka enacted a citizenship law disenfranchising precisely that section of the population that had played a critical role in the struggle against British rule: the Tamil plantation workers. Since independence, the Sinhala bourgeoisie has promoted racism against the Tamil minority as the principal means of diverting social antagonisms and preventing a unified movement of the working class.

The Chinese Revolution

103. In China, the nationalist movement took the form of a peasant uprising under the direct leadership of the Chinese Communist Party. After its disastrous defeat in 1927, the Communist Party retreated to the countryside and built up "red armies" with the support of sections of the peasantry. However it sought to justify its reorientation on practical and pragmatic grounds, the Communist Party's abandonment of its urban and proletarian foundations led to a profound change in its political and social character. The continuing adherence of the Chinese Stalinists to a Marxian phraseology did not alter the fact that the peasantry had become

their principal constituency. Significantly, Mao Zedong, who prior to the 1927 defeat had been on the right wing of the CCP, played the leading role in changing the strategic orientation and social base of the party.

104. Trotsky continued to carefully follow developments in China following his expulsion from the Russian Communist Party and Communist International in 1927. In a letter written in 1932 to supporters of the Left Opposition in China, he examined the implications of the political and sociological evolution of the CCP. Were the Communist Party to come to power on the basis of a peasant movement, its policies would, in the final analysis, he argued, reflect the interests and outlook of this social base. Trotsky foresaw the possibility of a conflict between the peasantry and the workers. "The peasant movement is a mighty revolutionary factor insofar as it is directed against the large landowners, militarists, feudalists, and usurers," he noted. "But in the peasant movement itself are very powerful proprietary and reactionary tendencies, and at a certain stage it can become hostile to the workers and sustain that hostility already equipped with arms. He who forgets about the dual nature of the peasantry is not a Marxist. The advanced workers must be taught to distinguish from among 'communist' labels and banners the actual social processes."[66]

105. When the Japanese occupation collapsed at the end of World War II, the CCP launched an offensive that led ultimately to the conquest of political power in October 1949. Mao's victory owed far less to his strategic "genius"—of which there was very little evidence either before or after 1949—than to a set of extraordinarily favorable conditions, created by the military collapse of the Japanese Empire. Moreover, the CCP sought repeatedly, even after the Japanese collapse, to negotiate some sort of settlement with Chiang Kai-shek and the Kuomintang. It was Chiang's intransigence, far less than Mao's determination, that blocked the path to compromise. The CCP reluctantly came to the conclusion that the overthrow of Chiang was necessary.

106. Mao's regime implemented bourgeois nationalist measures, including the expropriation of the landlord class, but it was intensely hostile to the working class. It brutally suppressed the Chinese Trotskyists, who had remained active within the urban proletarian centers in the af-

---

66 "Peasant War in China and the Proletariat," in: *Leon Trotsky on China*, p. 586.

termath of the 1927 defeat. After considerable equivocation, the regime took control of much of Chinese industry. The CCP established a bureaucratic police state along the Stalinist model, combining nationalization of industry and socialist rhetoric with an internal regime that ruthlessly suppressed opposition, particularly from the left. The nationalist policies of the CCP, including the so-called "Great Leap Forward," had disastrous consequences, including a famine that killed an estimated 30 million. On the international stage, Maoism perpetuated the Stalinist theory of an alliance with the bourgeoisie in backward countries, with disastrous consequences throughout Asia, including in Indonesia (where a million workers and peasants were slaughtered by the CIA-backed Indonesian military and anti-communist paramilitary forces in 1965-66) and in Vietnam (where the Stalinists brokered a partition in 1954 with French imperialism, setting the stage for the US intervention).

The Establishment of Israel

107. The principle of national-based politics and reform found a somewhat different expression in the formation of Israel in 1948, through the partition of the British protectorate of Palestine. The establishment of Israel as a Jewish state was viewed with sympathy by millions around the world who were repelled by the fascist horrors, including the extermination of nearly two thirds of European Jewry, that were just beginning to come to light. In objective terms, however, the creation of Israel was socially and politically reactionary, based on the principle of ethno-religious exclusion and the expropriation of Palestinians from their homeland. The state of Israel would later serve as the principal military garrison state defending the interests of American imperialism in the Middle East. This tragedy for both the Jewish and Arab populations was made possible by Stalinism, which, through its betrayals and its anti-Semitism, helped turn many socialist-minded Jews toward Zionism. In the 1920s, the Palestine Communist Party had fought for a unified movement of Jewish and Arab workers. However, the nationalist degeneration of the Stalinist parties found reflection in the PCP, which split into two sections along ethnic lines before the end of World War II. The Soviet bureaucracy completed

its betrayal of the working class of the region by supporting the creation of Israel as part of its post-war agreements with imperialism. In contrast, the Fourth International advanced an internationalist position based on the unification of the working class. It wrote in 1948:

> The Fourth International rejects as utopian and reactionary the "Zionist solution" of the Jewish question. It declares that total re-nunciation of Zionism is the sine qua non condition for the merging of Jewish workers' struggles with the social, national and liberationist struggles of the Arab toilers. It declares that to demand Jewish immigration into Palestine is thoroughly reactionary just as it is reactionary to call for immigration of any oppressor people into colonial countries in general. It holds that the question of immigration as well as the relations between Jews and Arabs can be decided adequately only after imperialism has been ousted by a freely elected Constituent Assembly with full rights for the Jews as a national minority.[67]

The Korean War

108. Next to the Chinese Revolution, the postwar anti-colonial upheavals found their most explosive expression in the outbreak of the Korean War in June 1950, in which the armed forces of North Korea, under Stalinist leadership, rapidly overwhelmed the army of the US-backed dictatorship of Syngman Rhee in South Korea. US President Truman ordered in the US military, under cover of a United Nations resolution, and reconquered most of the peninsula. As the US forces were approaching the Chinese border, Chinese troops entered the conflict, driving back the Americans; eventually the fighting stabilized along a line roughly corresponding to the prewar division. The American SWP placed the struggle in the context of the unfolding colonial revolution, rejecting claims that the Korean people were nothing more than puppets of Moscow. In an open

---

67 Second World Congress of the Fourth International, "Struggles of the Colonial Peoples and the World Revolution," *Fourth International*, July 1948, p. 157.

letter to the US government, Cannon declared, "The American intervention in Korea is a brutal imperialist invasion, no different from the French war on Indo-China or the Dutch assault on Indonesia. American boys are being sent 10,000 miles away to kill or be killed, not in order to liberate the Korean people, but to conquer and subjugate them. It is outrageous. It is monstrous." The Korean struggle "is part of the mighty uprising of the hundreds of millions of colonial people throughout Asia against western imperialism. This is the real truth, the real issue. The colonial slaves don't want to be slaves any longer."[68]

109. The Korean conflict clearly demonstrated the reactionary implications of the theories that the Soviet Union had become a new form of class society, either "bureaucratic collectivist" or "state capitalist." The theoretician of "bureaucratic collectivism," Max Shachtman, had broken with the Fourth International ten years earlier, promising to maintain an independent "third camp" position. But in 1950, he went over openly to the camp of American imperialism. Leaflets prepared by Shachtman's organization, by then called the Workers Party, were airdropped to Chinese and North Korean soldiers, giving them "socialist" arguments for surrendering to the American invaders. The leading proponent of the "state capitalist" view, Tony Cliff, broke with the Revolutionary Communist Party, then the British section of the Fourth International, which adhered to Cannon's uncompromising opposition to the imperialist war. Cliff adopted instead a position of strict neutrality, condemning what he called "Russian imperialism" equally with that of the United States.

The Origins of Pabloite Revisionism

110. The overall restabilization of capitalist development lent the postwar social struggles their contradictory character. The end of the war brought with it an upsurge of the class struggle in the advanced countries and the anti-imperialist movement in the colonies. However, the economic stabilization vastly expanded the field of operation for bourgeois national-

---

68 James P. Cannon, *Notebook of an Agitator* (New York: Pioneer Publishers, 1958), p. 186.

ist movements, Stalinists, trade union bureaucrats and various petty bourgeois tendencies that came to the head of these struggles. The objective function of these movements and organizations was, in one form or another, to provide a base of support within broader sections of the working class and oppressed masses for the maintenance of the global capitalist system. They encouraged the illusion that permanent gains could be realized through the policies of national reform that had been given a new lease on life following the war.

111. The complexities of the postwar period found expression in the form of a revisionist tendency within the Trotskyist movement that adapted to the bourgeois and petty bourgeois organizations. The revisionists came to see the Stalinist and Social-Democratic tendencies, as well as petty-bourgeois nationalist and radical movements, not as political obstacles to the independent mobilization of the working class, but, rather, as alternative instruments for realizing socialism. It was not, therefore, a matter of opposing to these organizations the independent perspective of the Fourth International, but rather of transforming the Fourth International into a pressure group on the existing leadership of the working class and national movements. The revisionists endowed the Stalinists and bourgeois nationalists with an historically progressive role, rejecting Trotsky's insistence on their counter-revolutionary character. This revision of the perspective upon which the founding of the Fourth International had been based was advanced initially by two leading figures in the post-war Trotskyist movement in Europe, Michel Pablo and Ernest Mandel.

112. Pablo's revisions were an impressionistic response to the political changes in Eastern Europe. The initial reaction of the Fourth International to the establishment of the Stalinist-dominated regimes was based on Trotsky's conceptions. Notwithstanding the political "successes" of the Stalinists, the Fourth International insisted on their essentially counter-revolutionary role. It stated in 1946:

> The unspeakable treacheries, their stamping out of mass uprising, their counterrevolutionary terror, their depredations and plunderings—these are discrediting in the eyes of the toilers the very word, the very idea of communism. How weighty are the East European nationalizations on the scales as against Stalin's crimes against the

working class? The Stalinist counterrevolutionary adventures in Eastern Europe, rather than endowing it with the aura of a progressive mission in history, have made more urgent the necessity of crushing this bloody fiend, and preventing it from doing any more damage than it has already done to the world working class and its struggle for emancipation.

The blindness of Stalinism, its unutterably reactionary character, its historical bankruptcy is exposed glaringly above all in Eastern Europe. For the sake of paltry loot, for the sake of the small change of reparations—completely meaningless so far as solving the USSR's economic needs—the Kremlin has raised against itself a wall of hatred throughout Eastern Europe and the world. For the sake of military control over the poverty-stricken, bankrupt Balkans, the Kremlin has helped the Anglo-American imperialists crush the revolution and prop up decaying capitalism.[69]

113.   In April 1949, the IEC of the Fourth International wrote:

An evaluation of Stalinism cannot be made on the basis of localized results of its policy but must proceed from the entirety of its actions on a world scale. When we consider the state of decay which capitalism presents even today, four years after the end of the war, and when we consider the concrete situation of 1943-45, there can be no doubt that Stalinism, on a world scale, appeared as the decisive factor in preventing a sudden and simultaneous crash of the capitalist order in Europe and in Asia. In this sense, the 'successes' achieved by the bureaucracy in the buffer zone constitute, at most, the price which imperialism paid for services rendered on the world arena—a price which is moreover constantly called into question at the following stage.

From the world point of view, the reforms realized by the Soviet bureaucracy in the sense of an assimilation of the buffer zone to the USSR weigh incomparably less in the balance than the blows dealt by the Soviet bureaucracy, especially through its actions in the buf-

---

fer zone, against the consciousness of the world proletariat, which it demoralizes, disorients and paralyzes by all its politics and thus renders it susceptible to some extent to the imperialist campaign of war preparations. Even from the point of view of the USSR itself, the defeats and the demoralization of the world proletariat caused by Stalinism constitute an incomparably greater danger than the consolidation of the buffer zone constitutes a reinforcement.[70]

Pablo's Repudiation of Trotskyism

114. But in the course of 1949 there were signs that Pablo was shifting his position. He began to write of the transition from capitalism to socialism taking place through "centuries" of "deformed workers' states" along the Stalinist model. In 1951, the International Executive Committee of the Fourth International passed a resolution supporting the theory of "war-revolution." This theory held that the eruption of war between the United States and the Soviet Union would assume the form of a global civil war, in which the Soviet bureaucracy would be compelled to serve as midwife for social revolutions. The same year, Pablo published a document arguing, "For our movement objective social reality consists essentially of the capitalist regime and the Stalinist world."[71]

115. Pablo's analysis wrote off the class conflict, the independent interests of the working class, and, therefore, the historical necessity of the Fourth International. For him, the task of the Fourth International was to function as a pressure group within the existing Stalinist organizations. Pabloism extended the false claims made on behalf of the Stalinist bureaucracy to the bourgeois nationalist movements in the semi-colonial and underdeveloped countries. In place of a class analysis, Pablo spoke of "integration into the real mass movement." In a report delivered to the Third World Congress of the FI in August-September 1951, he drew the conclusions of this perspective by declaring, "There is not now a single Trotskyist organization, which, either as a whole or in part, does not seriously, pro-

---

70 David North, *The Heritage We Defend*, pp. 158-59.

71 Cited in Ibid., p. 185.

foundly, concretely understand the necessity of subordinating all organizational considerations, of formal independence or otherwise, to real integration into the mass movement wherever it expresses itself in each country, or to integration in an important current of this movement which can be influenced."[72]

116. The theoretical foundation of Pabloism was an objectivist method that repudiated the emphasis placed by the Marxist movement on the role of the party in the development of the world revolution. As was later explained:

> The standpoint of objectivism is contemplation rather than revolutionary practical activity, of observation rather than struggle; it justifies what is happening rather than explains what must be done. This method provided the theoretical underpinnings for a perspective in which Trotskyism was no longer seen as the doctrine guiding the practical activity of a party determined to conquer power and change the course of history, but rather as a general interpretation of a historical process in which socialism would ultimately be realized under the leadership of nonproletarian forces hostile to the Fourth International. Insofar as Trotskyism was to be credited with any direct role in the course of events, it was merely as a sort of subliminal mental process unconsciously guiding the activities of Stalinists, neo-Stalinists, semi-Stalinists, and, of course, petty-bourgeois nationalists of one type or another.
>
> Pabloism, in this sense, went way beyond a set of incorrect assessments, false prognoses and programmatic revisions. It attacked the whole foundation of scientific socialism and repudiated the central lessons abstracted by Marxists from the development of the class struggle over an entire century. The greatest conquest of Marxist theory in the 20th century—the Leninist conception of the party— was undermined as Pablo called into question the necessity of the conscious element in the struggle of the proletariat and the historic realization of the proletarian dictatorship. For Pablo and his followers, there was no need to theoretically educate the working class and

---

make it conscious of its historical tasks. It was not necessary to wage a struggle for Marxism against the domination of bourgeois ideology over the spontaneous movement of the working class...

The adaptation to Stalinism was a central feature of the new Pabloite outlook, but it would be mistaken to see this as its essential characteristic. Pabloism was (and is) liquidationism all down the line: that is, the repudiation of the hegemony of the proletariat in the socialist revolution and the genuinely independent existence of the Fourth International as the conscious articulation of the historical role of the working class...

The practical activity of the Trotskyist movement was no longer to be centrally directed toward educating the proletariat, making it conscious of its historic tasks, and establishing its unconditional programmatic and organizational independence from all other class forces. Nor was this activity to be based upon a scientific analysis of social relations of production and class forces, grounded in a historically-based confidence in the unique revolutionary role of the proletariat. Instead, work was to be reduced to the small change of tactical expediency, in which principled positions established over decades of struggle were to be surrendered in the vain hope of influencing the leaders of the existing Stalinist, Social-Democratic and bourgeois nationalist organizations and pushing them to the left.[73]

117. Acting on this perspective, Pablo, with the support of Mandel, sought to exploit his position as International Secretary of the Fourth International to compel entire national sections to liquidate themselves as independent organizations and enter the ranks of the Stalinist parties, a tactic they called entryism *sui generis*. The revisionists concluded that the concentration that had been placed on the building of sections of the Fourth International in every country had been mistaken. This position became the hallmark of a disastrous perspective that would be repeated many times, including by innumerable opportunist tendencies today. It is not possible to build revolutionary parties, they conclude, so one must look

---

73 Ibid., pp. 188-91.

toward some other force that happens, at any given time, to be leading mass organizations, regardless of its history, program, and class basis.

118. The Pabloite tendency in the United States was led by Bert Cochran. It found support principally among a section of trade unionists inside the SWP, which reflected the pressures of anticommunism on the working class and the growth of a more conservative layer of workers that was benefiting from a rise in its standard of living. The Cochranites wanted to abandon any discussion of the split between Trotskyism and Stalinism, a position expressed in their infamous slogan, "Junk the Old Trotskyism." Opposing the basic principle that socialist consciousness is historical consciousness, Cochran wrote in 1951, "while Trotsky was, in the immediate and most direct sense, the teacher and the leader of our movement, it does not at all follow from these two propositions that we will have much success in rallying workers to our banner by trying to straighten them out on the rights and wrongs of the Stalin-Trotsky fight, which has now receded into history..."[74] This call to forget about history meant, in fact, rejecting the perspective and principles represented in that history. Most of the Cochranites would eventually take their liquidationist perspective to its logical conclusion by making their way into the trade union bureaucracy and the Democratic Party.

The "Open Letter" and the Formation of the International Committee

119. The factional struggle that developed in the Fourth International culminated in November 1953 with the issuing of an Open Letter, written by Cannon, to Trotskyists throughout the world. This letter formed the programmatic basis for the formation of the International Committee of the Fourth International. Supported by the Trotskyist organizations in France and Britain, Cannon's action was wholly justified by the circumstances that confronted the world movement. At stake was the defense of the essential political principles upon which the founding of the Fourth International had been based, and its survival as an independent revolu-

---

74 Cited in Ibid., p. 204.

tionary organization. Cannon's letter, in explaining why there could be no compromise with Pabloism, summarized these principles:

1. The death agony of the capitalist system threatens the destruction of civilization through worsening depressions, world wars and barbaric manifestations like fascism. The development of atomic weapons today underlines the danger in the gravest possible way.

2. The descent into the abyss can be avoided only by replacing capitalism with the planned economy of socialism on a world scale and thus resuming the spiral of progress opened up by capitalism in its early days.

3. This can be accomplished only under the leadership of the working class in society. But the working class itself faces a crisis in leadership although the world relationship of social forces was never so favorable as today for the workers to take the road to power.

4. To organize itself for carrying out this world-historic aim, the working class in each country must construct a revolutionary socialist party in the pattern developed by Lenin; that is, a combat party capable of dialectically combining democracy and centralism—democracy in arriving at decisions, centralism in carrying them out; a leadership controlled by the ranks, ranks able to carry forward under fire in disciplined fashion.

5. The main obstacle to this is Stalinism, which attracts workers through exploiting the prestige of the October 1917 Revolution in Russia, only later, as it betrays their confidence, to hurl them either into the arms of the Social Democracy, into apathy, or back into illusions in capitalism. The penalty for these betrayals is paid by the working people in the form of consolidation of fascist or monarchist forces, and new outbreaks of war fostered and prepared by capitalism. From its inception, the Fourth International set as one of its major tasks the revolutionary overthrow of Stalinism inside and outside the USSR.

6. The need for flexible tactics facing many sections of the Fourth International, and parties or groups sympathetic to its program, makes it all the more imperative that they know how to fight imperialism and all its petty-bourgeois agencies (such as nationalist formations or trade union bureaucracies) without capitulation to

Stalinism; and, conversely, know how to fight Stalinism (which in the final analysis is a petty-bourgeois agency of imperialism) without capitulating to imperialism.[75]

120. The Open Letter pointed out that all these principles had been rejected by Pablo:

> ...In place of emphasizing the danger of a new barbarism, he sees the drive toward socialism as "irreversible"; yet he does not see socialism coming within our generation or some generations to come. Instead he has advanced the concept of an "engulfing" wave of revolutions that give birth to nothing but "deformed," that is, Stalin-type workers' states which are to last for "centuries."
>
> This reveals the utmost pessimism about the capacities of the working class, which is wholly in keeping with the ridicule he has lately voiced of the struggle to build independent revolutionary socialist parties. In place of holding to the main course of building independent revolutionary socialist parties by all tactical means, he looks to the Stalinist bureaucracy, or a decisive section of it, to so change itself under mass pressure as to accept the "ideas" and "program" of Trotskyism.[76]

121. Cannon's letter ended with a warning and a call to action:

> To sum up: The lines of cleavage between Pablo's revisionism and orthodox Trotskyism are so deep that no compromise is possible either politically or organizationally. The Pablo faction has demonstrated that it will not permit democratic decisions truly reflecting majority opinion to be reached. They demand complete submission to their criminal policy. They are determined to drive all orthodox Trotskyists out of the Fourth International or to muzzle and handcuff them. ...

---

75 "The *Open Letter* of the Socialist Workers Party, November 16, 1953," in: *Trotskyism Versus Revisionism*, Volume One (London: New Park, 1974) pp. 299-300.

76 Ibid., p. 301.

If we may offer advice to the sections of the Fourth International from our enforced position outside the ranks[77], we think the time has come to act and act decisively. The time has come for the orthodox Trotskyist majority of the Fourth International to assert their will against Pablo's usurpation of authority.[78]

The Lenin-Trotsky Theory of the Party

122.   In the aftermath of the split, Cannon elaborated on the essential issues of principle that had emerged. He stressed the irreconcilable opposition of Marxism to the spontaneist conceptions of Pablo and Mandel:

> ...We alone are unconditional adherents of the Lenin-Trotsky theory of the party of the conscious vanguard and its role as leader of the revolutionary struggle. This theory acquires burning actuality and dominates all others in the present epoch.
>
> The problem of leadership now is not limited to spontaneous manifestations of the class struggle in a long drawn-out process, nor even to the conquest of power in this or that country where capitalism is especially weak. It is a question of the development of the international revolution and the socialist transformation of society. To admit that this can happen automatically is, in effect, to abandon Marxism altogether. No, it can only be a conscious operation, and it imperatively requires the leadership of the Marxist party which represents the conscious element in the historic process. No other party will do. No other tendency in the labor movement can be recognized as a satisfactory substitute. For that reason, our attitude towards all other parties and tendencies is irreconcilably hostile.
>
> If the relation of forces requires the adaptation of the cadres of the vanguard to organizations dominated at the moment by such hostile tendencies—Stalinist, Social-Democratic, centrist—then such

---

77   The American Trotskyists since the 1940s have not been able to affiliate formally with the Fourth International due to the provisions of the reactionary Voorhis Act.

78   Ibid., pp. 312-13.

adaptation must be regarded at all times as a tactical adaptation, to facilitate the struggle against them; never to effect a reconciliation with them; never to ascribe to them the decisive historical role, with the Marxists assigned to the minor chore of giving friendly advice and "loyal" criticism...[79]

Stalinism in Crisis

123. The struggle within the Fourth International both reflected and anticipated changes in the world situation. Even as the split was unfolding, the Kremlin regime was gripped by crisis. The bloody purge trials in Eastern Europe and the infamous arrests of Jewish physicians in the Soviet Union made it all too clear, even within Stalin's entourage, that the dictator's raging paranoia was blocking any coherent policy response to the crisis of post-war Soviet society. Stalin's sudden death in March 1953, under murky circumstances, created an opportunity for a shift in policy. After a brief factional battle within the Politburo, Lavrenti Beria, the head of Stalin's secret police, was ousted from power and executed. With this act, the bureaucracy, which owed its power to Stalin's destruction of the revolutionary cadre of the Bolshevik Party, expressed its desire to enjoy its privileges without the ever-present danger of purges, arrests and executions. But the bureaucracy's hold on its privileges faced a greater challenge from the growing discontent of the working class within the Soviet Union and in Eastern Europe. In June 1953, workers in East Germany rose up against the Stalinist bureaucracy and were suppressed by Soviet military forces. In February 1956, Nikita Khrushchev delivered his "secret speech" to the Twentieth Congress of the Communist Party, in which he denounced some of Stalin's crimes, but deliberately excluded from his list of victims the leaders of the Trotskyist Left Opposition and those condemned to death at the Moscow Trials. As the leader of the Stalinist bureaucracy, Khrushchev could not give an account of the origins of Stalin's crimes and resorted to a facile apology: Stalin's henchmen in the bureaucracy and the entire

---

79 Letter from Cannon to George Breitman, March 1, 1954, in *Trotskyism Versus Revisionism*, Volume Two (London: New Park, 1974) p. 65.

Soviet population had been in thrall of a "cult of personality." That same year, the Hungarian working class revolted, setting up workers' councils that were the embryonic form of a political revolution. The uprising was brutally suppressed as Khrushchev sent Soviet tanks into Budapest. This action revealed once more the thoroughly counter-revolutionary character of Stalinism. The unrelenting opposition of Stalinism to any revolutionary movement of the working class had not been altered by the death of Stalin himself.

124. The crisis of Stalinism provided a real possibility for the clarification of central political questions. The British Trotskyists, under the leadership of Gerry Healy, stressed the importance of clarifying the great political issues that underlay Trotsky's struggle against Stalinism. This entailed deepening the struggle against the Pabloites, who interpreted every Stalinist political maneuver as an example of progressive bureaucratic "self-reform." It was precisely at this point, however, that the SWP leadership began to retreat from the irreconcilable opposition to Pabloism that Cannon had advocated so forcefully in 1953-54. By 1957, Cannon was expressing interest in the possibility of a reunification with the Pabloites, on the false grounds that differences between the ICFI and the Pabloite Secretariat had diminished over the years. This shift in the attitude of the SWP toward the Pabloites reflected a definite rightward drift in its general political line. In the late 1950s, the SWP indicated interest in participating in a "regroupment" of various radical tendencies. The turn to the Pabloites expressed a shift in the class axis of the SWP, away from its traditional "proletarian orientation" and toward alliances with political representatives of the radical sections of the petty bourgeoisie.

Castroism and the SWP's Return to Pablo

125. The accession of Castro to power in Cuba in January 1959 became a vehicle for the growing opportunist faction within the SWP to reorient the party back toward the petty-bourgeois milieu of American radicalism. The Castro government had come to power with a bourgeois nationalist program through guerrilla warfare based on the peasantry. The nationalist character of the movement, and its initial efforts to implement

social reforms, brought it into conflict with American imperialism. Castro, in response to US threats, sought support from the Soviet Union. Only at this point did the regime declare itself to be "Communist."

126. Though it had initially defined the Castro regime as bourgeois nationalist, the SWP, now led by Joseph Hansen, shifted its position in the course of 1960. A key role in the implementation of this change was the SWP's intense and politically unexplained involvement with the dubious "Fair Play for Cuba Committee." By December 1960, the SWP was declaring that Cuba had become a workers' state. Hansen defended this position on the crudely empiricist basis that nationalized property had been established, apparently unaware that land nationalization—as Lenin had frequently noted in his voluminous writings on the agrarian question in Russia—is, in essence, a bourgeois democratic measure. Nor did Hansen reference the analysis of Cuban developments to the historical and theoretical problems—including the class basis of the regime and the absence of independent organizations of working class power—that had preoccupied the SWP in the discussions over Eastern Europe and China. Moreover, the developments in Cuba were treated in isolation from the international situation and all questions of global perspective. The "fact" that Castro had carried out nationalizations was proof, the SWP argued, that a revolution could be accomplished with a "blunted instrument" led by "unconscious Marxists," who would implement socialism due to the pressure of objective necessity and without the active participation of the working class itself.

127. The SWP's position, which closely paralleled the argument of the Pabloites, repudiated the principles outlined by Cannon in his Open Letter. If workers' states could be established through the actions of petty-bourgeois guerrilla leaders based on the peasantry, and under conditions in which there existed no identifiable organs of working class rule, then what was the purpose of the Fourth International? What need was there to organize the working class politically on the basis of a socialist program? The SWP's adulation of Castroism and guerrilla warfare in Latin America was a rejection of a revolutionary perspective for the American and international working class. Its position on Cuba went hand in hand with the party's increasing adaptation to middle class protest politics in the US.

The SLL's Defense of Trotskyism

128. These developments intensified the political conflict within the International Committee. In a letter dated January 2, 1961, the Socialist Labour League, the British section of the ICFI, wrote to the SWP leadership:

> The greatest danger confronting the revolutionary movement is liquidationism, flowing from a capitulation either to the strength of imperialism or of the bureaucratic apparatuses in the Labour movement, or both. Pabloism represents, even more clearly now than in 1953, this liquidationist tendency in the international Marxist movement…
>
> Any retreat from the strategy of political independence of the working class and the construction of revolutionary parties will take on the significance of a world-historical blunder on the part of the Trotskyist movement…
>
> It is because of the magnitude of the opportunities opening up before Trotskyism, and therefore the necessity for political and theoretical clarity, that we urgently require a drawing of the lines against revisionism in all its forms. It is time to draw to a close the period in which Pabloite revisionism was regarded as a trend within Trotskyism. Unless this is done we cannot prepare for the revolutionary struggles now beginning.[80]

129. In May 1961 the SLL expanded its critique of the SWP's retreat from Trotskyism and its ever-more pronounced adaptation to the myriad bourgeois and petty-bourgeois nationalist tendencies that dominated the anti-colonial and anti-imperialist movements. The line of the SWP, as the SLL documents established, represented a repudiation of the conceptions elaborated by Trotsky in his Theory of Permanent Revolution:

> An essential of revolutionary Marxism in this epoch is the theory that the national bourgeoisie in under-developed countries is inca-

---

80 Letter of the National Committee of the SLL to the National Committee of the SWP January 2, 1961, in *Trotskyism Versus Revisionism Volume Three* (London: New Park, 1974) pp. 48-49.

pable of defeating imperialism and establishing an independent national state. This class has ties with imperialism and it is of course incapable of an independent capitalist development, for it is part of the capitalist world market and cannot compete with the products of the advanced countries...

While it is true that the stage of 'independence' reached by countries like Ghana, and the national independence movements led by men like Mboya of Kenya, acts as a stimulant to national liberation movements in other countries, the fact remains that Nkrumah, Mboya, Nasser, Kassem, Nehru, Soekarno, and their like, represent the national bourgeoisie of their own countries. The dominant imperialist policy-makers both in the USA and Britain recognize full well that only by handing over political 'independence' to leaders of this kind, or accepting their victory over feudal elements like Farouk and Nuries-Said, can the stakes of international capital and the strategic alliances be preserved in Asia, Africa, and Latin America...

It is not the job of Trotskyists to boost the role of such nationalist leaders. They can command the support of the masses only because of the betrayal of leadership by Social-Democracy and particularly Stalinism, and in this way they become buffers between imperialism and the mass of workers and peasants. The possibility of economic aid from the Soviet Union often enables them to strike a harder bargain with the imperialists, even enables more radical elements among the bourgeois and petty-bourgeois leaders to attack imperialist holdings and gain further support from the masses. But, for us, in every case the vital question is one of the working class in these countries gaining political independence through a Marxist party, leading the poor peasantry to the building of Soviets, and recognizing the necessary connections with the international socialist revolution. In no case, in our opinion, should Trotskyists substitute for that the hope that the nationalist leadership should become socialists. The emancipation of the working class is the task of the workers themselves.[81]

130. On the question of Cuba, the SLL added:

---

81 *The Heritage We Defend*, op. cit., pp. 377-79.

Much of the current discussion on Cuba, it seems, proceeds in this way: The Cuban masses support Castro; Castro began as a petty-bourgeois but has become a socialist; the public pressure of imperialist attack and of popular struggle may turn him into a Marxist, and already the tasks confronting him in defending the gains of the revolution have brought him 'naturally' to positions indistinguishable from Trotskyism. In this approach, the fundamentals of Marxism are trampled upon...[W]e have to evaluate political tendencies on a class basis, on the way they develop in struggle in relation to the movement of classes over long periods. A proletarian party, let alone a proletarian revolution, will not be born in any backward country by the conversion of petty-bourgeois nationalists who stumble 'naturally' and 'accidentally' upon the importance of workers and peasants.[82]

The Pabloite Reunification and the Betrayal in Ceylon

131. In June 1963, the SWP and the European Pabloites held a Unification Congress and formed a new "United Secretariat." What imparted to this congress its unprincipled and reactionary character, was its determined refusal to examine the issues that had led to the split of 1953. The repeated claim that the differences had receded into the past, that they were no longer relevant in the context of a "new world reality," concealed the very real and dangerous implications of Pabloite politics. The refusal of the British Trotskyists to participate in the reactionary charade of a "Reunification" Congress, in which life-and-death questions were being excluded from discussion, was an act of great political courage.

132. Just what was at stake became clear within just one year. In June 1964, a leading section of the Pabloite International, the Lanka Sama Samaja Party (LSSP), accepted an invitation from Ceylonese Prime Minister Madam Sirimavo Bandaranaike to join her new bourgeois coalition government. This was the first time in the history of the Fourth International that a Trotskyist party had participated in such a crass be-

---

82   Ibid., p. 379.

trayal of socialist principles. This betrayal had been prepared over many years of political backsliding by the LSSP, but the Pabloites blocked discussion of its political degeneration. Now, just one year after reunification, the Pabloite International (with the critical assistance of the SWP) was serving as the midwife of a betrayal that led to a civil war that has ravaged Sri Lankan society and cost nearly 100,000 lives. The condemnation issued by the International Committee of the role played by Pabloism in the Ceylonese catastrophe has stood the test of time: "The entry of the LSSP members into the Bandaranaike coalition marks the end of a whole epoch of the evolution of the Fourth International. It is in direct service to imperialism, in the preparation of a defeat for the working class that revision in the world Trotskyist movement has found its expression."[83]

Opposition in the SWP: The Emergence of the ACFI

133. Within the Socialist Workers Party, a minority tendency, led by Tim Wohlforth, opposed the increasingly opportunist orientation of the SWP and supported the criticisms made by the Socialist Labour League. The greatest strength of this tendency was its recognition that the political crisis of the SWP had to be approached as an international problem. The struggle within the SWP, therefore, could not be conducted from the standpoint of obtaining a tactical advantage in the discussion of one or another political issue. Instead, the basic aim of the discussion was to achieve political and theoretical clarification of the central problems of revolutionary perspective in the Fourth International. The advice given by the British SLL to its American supporters was to avoid, to the greatest extent possible, factional conflicts over secondary political differences and organizational issues, and to work for the political clarification of the SWP cadre. This principled approach differed sharply from that taken by another minority tendency, led by James Robertson, which placed its national factional concerns above those of international clarification.

134. The Wohlforth-led minority worked within the SWP from 1961 to 1964. Even after the 1963 Reunification Congress, the minority continued

---

83 *The Heritage We Defend*, op. cit., p. 402.

to seek a principled political discussion within the Socialist Workers Party. However, events in Ceylon brought the struggle within the SWP to a head. The pro-ICFI minority issued a letter to the SWP membership demanding that the organization permit a discussion of the roots of the LSSP's betrayal. The statement issued in June 1964 by the minority declared:

> During the whole period from 1961 to 1963 we reiterated time and time again, in political solidarity with the International Committee, that a reunification of the Fourth International without the fullest political discussion prior to the actual reunification could only lead to disaster and the further disintegration of the international movement and the party here. Our position has been fully vindicated…
>
> There can no longer be any further refusal to face up to the political, theoretical and methodological crisis tearing apart our party and the international formation to which it is presently in political solidarity. For the very survival of the party a thoroughgoing discussion of these questions must be organized immediately in all branches.[84]

135.   After issuing this letter, all nine signatories were suspended from membership. The minority formed the American Committee for the Fourth International and undertook the extensive preparations necessary for the transformation of the ACFI into a new Trotskyist party, allied politically with the International Committee.

The Third Congress of the ICFI

136.   In the aftermath of the reunification, the ICFI had to assess the lessons of the struggle against Pabloism and its objective significance. The International Committee held its Third World Congress in April 1966 to consolidate the forces of World Trotskyism and lay the foundations for constructing Trotskyist parties throughout the world. The Congress resolution pointed to the contradictions within world imperialism and the signs of a decline of the postwar boom. It noted:

---

84   *The Heritage We Defend*, op. cit., p. 403.

Imperialism is in a deepening crisis. The development of the productive forces during and since World War Two, particularly the
production of nuclear weapons and the introduction of automation,
strains to breaking point the conflict between the productive forces
and capitalist property relations. The struggles produced by this
contradiction radicalize the working class youth. The parties of the
Fourth International will be built through these struggles.

137.   The Congress resolution emphasized the objective role of Pabloite
revisionism in blocking the revolutionary upsurge of the working class:

Revisionism, which separates into distinct sectors the revolution
in the advanced countries, the "colonial revolution," and the political
revolution in the workers' states, is a most important cover for capitalist domination of the workers' movement and for obstructing the
construction of revolutionary parties. This revisionism is expressed
particularly in the theory and practice of the self-styled Unified
Secretariat of the Fourth International, which was formed without
discussion of theoretical and political questions. The next phase in
the building of the Fourth International must on the contrary be accompanied by a most serious theoretical discussion in all sections of
the policies and theory of the movement, past and present.[85]

138.   The International Committee stressed the necessity of basing the
development of the Fourth International on the lessons of past struggles. It
also insisted that the fight against Pabloite revisionism was a politically and
theoretically decisive element of the history of the Fourth International—
not a diversion from other, more important, tasks of party building. It was
precisely in the persistent struggle against the revision of Marxism that
the Trotskyist movement fought the ideological pressures exerted by the
bourgeoisie and developed its revolutionary perspective. This conception
of the historical and political implications of the struggle against revisionism was opposed by two tendencies that had been invited to the Third

85 "Resolution of the Third World Conference, April 8, 1966," in: *Trotskyism Versus
Revisionism*, Volume 5 (London: New Park Publications, 1975), pp. 25-27.

Congress, in order to determine whether principled political collaboration was possible—Voix Ouvrière and James Robertson's Spartacist tendency. In both cases, it proved not to be possible.

139. According to these groups, the ICFI vastly overestimated the significance of Pabloism and the political struggles within the Fourth International. Robertson declared at the 1966 conference:

> We take issue with the notion that the present crisis of capitalism is so sharp and deep that Trotskyist revisionism is needed to tame the workers, in a way comparable to the degeneration of the Second and Third Internationals. Such an erroneous estimation would have as its point of departure an enormous overestimation of our present significance, and would accordingly be disorienting.[86]

140. All that divides Marxism, theoretically and politically, from petty-bourgeois radicalism was summed up in this statement. In essence, Robertson denied the objective social and political significance of the conflict within the Fourth International. The lessons of Lenin's struggle to build the Bolshevik Party in the struggle against revisionism, and, later, of Trotsky's struggle against Stalinism and various forms of centrism, were ignored. The struggle against Pabloism within the Fourth International —so clearly connected to major political and social processes in the aftermath of World War II—was derided by Robertson as a subjectively-motivated squabble between various individuals. And Robertson's evaluation came less than two years after the entry of the LSSP into a bourgeois coalition government!

Pabloism, the New Left and Guerrillaism

141. Even as Robertson made these comments, the Pabloites were setting in place props and buffers upon which both the bourgeoisie and the Stalinists would rely in the social upheavals that were approaching. In the United States, the SWP was playing a critical role in the subordination of

---

86 "Spartacist Statement to the International Conference, *Marxist Internet Archive*, http://www.marxistsfr.org/history/etol/document/icl-spartacists/1986/1966conf.html

the growing anti-Vietnam War movement to the capitalist Democratic Party. Throughout Europe, the Pabloite organizations were adapting themselves to both the Stalinists and the petty-bourgeois "New Left" tendencies that were soon to contribute significantly to diverting and disorienting the mass movements of social protest that erupted in 1968. In France, the Pabloites facilitated the Stalinist betrayal of the revolutionary eruption of the working class in May-June of that year. And further, as the Czechoslovak "Prague Spring" of 1968 and the wave of strikes in Poland clearly demonstrated, the Stalinist regimes were already entering into terminal crisis. The Pabloite organizations, with their theories of self-reforming bureaucracies, diverted the Fourth International from concentrating its forces in an implacable struggle against the Stalinist regimes and preparing for their overthrow. It was not pre-determined, in the mid-1960s, that the eventual collapse of Stalinism would lead inexorably to the formation of right-wing and pro-capitalist regimes in the USSR and Eastern Europe. Indeed, in the 1960s, the struggles against Stalinist tyranny in Eastern Europe were left-wing and socialist. The later reactionary outcome in Eastern Europe, the USSR and, for that matter, China, was the product of political conditions that were shaped, to a significant extent, by the Pabloites' false and reactionary policies.

142. Among the betrayals of Pabloism was its glorification of Castroism and guerrillaism, which had a devastating impact on an entire generation of left-wing workers and youth in Latin America. The political disasters of the 1970s—in Chile, Argentina, Bolivia and Uruguay—were the consequence of theories and policies promoted by the Pabloite United Secretariat. The signal for the repudiation of Trotskyism was given by the United Secretariat's celebration of Ernesto "Che" Guevara, the Argentine radical who, like many Latin American intellectuals of his generation, explicitly rejected the Marxist conception of the revolutionary role of the working class. The Pabloites looked the other way when Guevara welcomed Ramon Mercader, the assassin of Trotsky, to Cuba after the latter's release from a Mexican prison in 1960. They called on socialist youth in Latin America to find an alternative to a strategy based on the working class. As the Bolivian Pabloite Moscoso wrote:

> The guerrilla method advocated by the Cubans is applicable to all underdeveloped countries, although its form must vary in ac-

cord with the peculiarities of each country. In those countries where there exists a great peasant mass with an unresolved land problem, the guerrillas will draw their strength from the peasantry; the guerrilla struggle will bring this mass into action, solving their agrarian problem arms in hand, as occurred in Cuba, starting from the Sierra Maestra. But in other countries the proletariat and the radicalized petty bourgeoisie of the cities will provide the guerrilla forces.[87]

"Continuity" vs. "Reconstruction" of the Fourth International

143. The ICFI—and, in particular, the British Trotskyists of the Socialist Labour League—demonstrated great political prescience at the 1966 Congress and its aftermath in opposing all efforts to denigrate the fight against Pabloite revisionism. "The first prerequisite is to grasp that the fight against Pabloism was a fight to develop Marxism and at the same time to defend every past conquest of Marxist theory," the SLL wrote in 1967. "The 1966 Conference of the IC expressed this clearly in insisting that the IC, through its struggle inside the FI, represented the continuity of the movement. Against Voix Ouvrière and Robertson, we insisted that only in the fight against Pabloism had Marxists preserved and developed the theory of the revolutionary party, of Bolshevism."[88]

144. The French section of the Fourth International, the Organisation Communiste Internationaliste (OCI) supported the position of the SLL at the 1966 Congress. However, it argued that the Fourth International had to be "reconstructed." Underlying this ambiguous terminology—which betrayed a significant degree of skepticism toward the viability of the Fourth International as it had emerged out of the break with the Pabloites—was a centrist shift in the OCI itself. By 1967, the OCI had begun to insist that the main problem with Pabloism was not its orientation to Stalinism and bourgeois nationalism, but its overly centralized bureaucratic methods.

---

87   Hugo González Moscoso, "The Cuban Revolution and Its Lessons," in: *Fifty Years of World Revolution*, ed. Ernest Mandel [New York: Pathfinder Press, 1970], pp. 194-95.

88   "Reply to the OCI by the Central Committee of the SLL, June 19, 1967" in *Trotskyism Versus Revisionism Volume Five* (London: New Park, 1975) p. 111.

The OCI insisted that the task was to build more "supple" organizations focused on the "united front" tactic. The SLL issued a prescient warning to the OCI leadership:

> Now the radicalization of the workers in Western Europe is proceeding rapidly, particularly in France... There is always a danger at such a stage of development that a revolutionary party responds to the situation in the working class not in a revolutionary way, but by adaptation to the level of struggle to which the workers are restricted by their own experience under the old leaderships, i.e., to the inevitable initial confusion. Such revisions of the fight for the independent Party and the Transitional Program are usually dressed up in the disguise of getting closer to the working class, unity with all those in struggle, not posing ultimatums, abandoning dogmatism, etc.[89]

The Formation of the Workers League

145. Based on the lessons of the Third Congress, the American Committee for the Fourth International completed its preparation for the establishment of a new Trotskyist party, in political solidarity with the ICFI. The founding congress of the Workers League took place in November 1966. The growing opposition to the war in Vietnam among masses of students, the eruption of violent protests by African-American workers and youth in major cities, and the militant strikes by substantial sections of the working class were indications of the crisis of American capitalism. The Socialist Workers Party, repudiating its Trotskyist heritage, responded to these developments by adapting to petty-bourgeois tendencies that dominated these movements. Its opportunism found expression in its promotion of Black nationalism as an alternative to the struggle for the unity of the working class on the basis of a socialist program. The SWP's espousal of Black nationalism, including the demand for a separate Black nation, reflected its dismissal of the American working class as a rev-

---

89 Ibid., pp. 113-14.

olutionary force. This perspective expressed the influence of the New Left, which derived much of its theoretical inspiration from the anti-Marxist conceptions of Herbert Marcuse, a leading representative of the "Frankfurt School," who characterized the working class as a "proto-fascist" element in American society.

146. The founding of the Workers League, rooted in the struggles of the Fourth International since 1953, marked a milestone in the fight for Marxism in the United States. The development of Marxism could only proceed on the basis of the recognition of the revolutionary character of the American working class and its decisive role in the struggle against US imperialism. This perspective could be realized only on the basis of an irreconcilable struggle against the myriad petty-bourgeois radical tendencies, promoting various forms of racial, ethnic, sexual and gender "identity" politics, that flourished in the 1960s and early 1970s. In his greetings to the Workers League's founding congress, SLL leader Gerry Healy stated:

> The working class in the United States is the most powerful in the world, and it is within this class that you must build your party. This is a basic principle of Marxism and one which applies with particular urgency to the conditions existing inside the United States. It is not Black Power or the dozens of peace and civil rights movements which extend throughout the country which will resolve the basic questions of our time, but the working class led by a revolutionary party. It is at this point that we separate ourselves completely from the revisionists. We emphatically reject their idea that the Negroes by themselves as well as middle-class movements can settle accounts with American imperialism. Whatever critical support we are called upon from time to time to extend to such movements, the essence of our support must be based on making clear our criticisms of their shortcomings.[90]

147. The central task confronting the Workers League was to fight for the political independence of the American working class from the bour-

---

90 *The Fourth International and the Renegade Wohlforth* (New York: Labor Publications, 1984), p. 209.

geoisie and its political parties, especially the Democratic Party. This assumed the form of the demand, in the conditions then prevailing in the United States, that the mass trade union organizations of the AFL-CIO form a labor party based on socialist policies. This demand, which arose out of the experiences of the 1930s, and which had been initially proposed by Trotsky, had been largely abandoned by the SWP in the 1950s, as it reoriented itself to the middle-class protest movements. It was revived by the Workers League, which declared, in its principal resolution at the founding congress:

> The working class must be shown that it must of necessity go beyond isolated economic struggles to a fundamental political struggle against the ruling class and its political instruments. The labor party demand thus becomes the unifying demand of all our work in the United States. It must permeate all our propaganda and agitation: among the working class youth, in the trade unions, among the minority peoples, around the war question...
>
> We must struggle for a labor party which will unite black and white workers in a common struggle against the common oppressor rather than concede to race politics. The concept of a labor party must be taken into the anti-war movement. The struggle against the war policies of the US imperialists cannot be separated from the other anti-working class policies of the imperialists. Middle class political parties set up on a "classless" basis to fight the "war issue" are futile efforts and serve to obscure the class issues involved rather than to explain them.[91]

148. The fight for the formation of a labor party, based on the trade unions, would play a major role in the struggle waged by the Workers League, over the next 25 years, against the subordination of the working class by the AFL-CIO bureaucracy to the Democratic Party. This demand was not conceived as a proposal for the building of a reformist alternative to the revolutionary party—i.e., an American version of the British Labour

---

91 Quoted from M. McLaughlin, *Vietnam and the World Revolution* (Detroit: Labor Publications, 1985), p. 96.

Party or the Canadian New Democratic Party—but as a means of developing a revolutionary political movement of the working class and breaking the stranglehold of class collaborationist policies. Moreover, as long as the AFL-CIO functioned, even if in only a limited way, as an instrument of working class struggles, and commanded the allegiance of significant sections of class conscious workers, the demand for the building of a labor party, committed to socialist policies, provided a clear political lead to the working class, indicated a path beyond the limits of trade unionism, and played a significant role in the development of revolutionary and socialist class consciousness. Later, changes of an objective character in the nature of the trade unions and their relationship to the working class—the product of developments in the structure of global capitalism and the cumulative impact of massive betrayals of working class struggles by the trade unions—would compel the Workers League to withdraw its demand for the labor party.

149.   The escalating conflict between Trotskyism and revisionism unfolded against the backdrop of increasing economic and political instability. The overwhelming economic preponderance of the United States at the end of World War II—which was critical for the restabilization and reconstruction of world capitalism—eroded in the course of the 1950s and 1960s. The export of American capital overseas had, by the 1960s, produced a dollar crisis that signaled the breakdown of the postwar equilibrium. Repeated efforts to contain the crisis proved futile, and on August 15, 1971, the United States destroyed the foundation of the Bretton Woods system by ending dollar-gold convertibility. The Socialist Labour League recognized that the breakdown of the Bretton Woods systems would lead to new economic and political convulsions, but unresolved issues within the International Committee, and within the SLL itself, would soon begin to exact a heavy political toll.

Split in the International Committee

150.   The growth of the British and French sections in the aftermath of the Third Congress of the ICFI—and especially after the events of May-June 1968—led to political conflict. But while the British section made

correct criticisms of the centrist orientation of the OCI, political differences were emerging within the Socialist Labour League leadership itself. Though it was known that Cliff Slaughter, who held the position of ICFI secretary, had evinced sympathy with the OCI's call for a "reconstruction" of the Fourth International, the issue was not pursued within the leadership. A similarly evasive attitude was taken toward the uncritical attitude of Michael Banda, another leading member of the SLL, toward Mao's "Cultural Revolution" and the policies of the National Liberation Front in Vietnam. The reluctance of the SLL leadership to engage in an open discussion of these vital issues reflected Healy's anxiety that political conflict within his own organization would undermine the practical work and organizational advances being made by the British section.

151. The avoidance of an examination of crucial questions of perspectives—essential for the development of political program—assumed within the Socialist Labour League a peculiar theoretical form. As differences with the OCI intensified in 1970-71, the SLL leadership argued that the political issues in dispute were merely secondary, even inessential, manifestations of differences over philosophy. The significant truth that philosophical method is revealed in the exercise of political analysis was invoked in a one-sided manner, to justify the dissolution of the concrete examination of political issues into ever-more abstract discussions of philosophical epistemology. When the OCI asserted, incorrectly, that dialectical materialism was not a "theory of knowledge," this was seized on to shift attention away from an examination of the French organization's centrist politics. In contrast to the approach taken by Trotsky in the 1939-40 struggle against Burnham and Shachtman—in which the significance and proper use of the dialectical materialist method was clearly related to questions of political perspective—Healy and Slaughter advanced the position that the discussion of dialectics superseded the political issues and even rendered them superfluous.

152. In the autumn of 1971, the SLL announced a split in the Fourth International, while leaving the political issues unclarified. Despite the plethora of crucial political questions, bound up with problems of revolutionary strategy arising from the crisis of capitalism and struggles of the working class, the SLL declared, in a statement published on March 1, 1972, that the split was "not about tactical aspects of how to build the

Fourth International. ... the split is not a question of dozens of detailed points of organization, or even of political positions on various questions." Rather, the SLL asserted, "It is a political split, going to the foundations of the Fourth International—Marxist theory."[92] But without the necessary elaboration of the actual political issues in dispute, the invocation of "Marxist theory" was little more than an exercise in abstract rhetoric. The SLL wrote that it had learned "from experience of building the revolutionary party in Britain that a thoroughgoing and difficult struggle against idealist ways of thinking was necessary which went much deeper than questions of agreement on program and policy."[93] This statement directly contradicted Trotsky, who held that "The significance of the program is the significance of the party," and that this program consisted of "a common understanding of events, of the tasks..."[94] Now the SLL was claiming that the "struggle against idealist ways of thinking"—a rather vague formulation—was more important than programmatic agreement! Moreover, the SLL's assertion that it was basing its work on the experience "of building the revolutionary party in Britain", rather than on the lessons of the Fourth International's struggle against Stalinism, Social Democracy and Pabloism, expressed a disturbing shift in its political axis—from internationalism to nationalism.

153.   This failure to clarify the political issues that underlay the split with the OCI undermined the work of the International Committee at precisely the point when the crisis of world capitalism required the greatest possible degree of programmatic clarity. The principal task confronting the leadership of the Socialist Labour League was to draw out the implications of the centrist drift in the program, practice and international orientation of the OCI. This was of the greatest importance at a time when new sections of the International Committee were being formed. The Revolutionary Communist League was established as the Ceylonese section in 1968. The Bund Sozialistischer Arbeiter was established as the

---

92   "Statement by the International Committee (Majority), March 1, 1972," in: *Trotskyism Versus Revisionism*, Volume Six [London: New Park, 1975], pp. 72 and 78.

93   Ibid., p. 83.

94   Leon Trotsky, *The Transitional Program for Socialist Revolution* (New York: Pathfinder, 2001), pp. 207-08.

German section in 1971. The Socialist Labor League was established as the Australian section in 1972. In Greece, the establishment of a new section in 1972 occurred under conditions in which its membership had been divided between supporters of the ICFI and the OCI.

154. It has now become publicly known that, in the late 1960s and early 1970s, the OCI became heavily involved in the behind-the-scenes political maneuvers that led to the creation of the French Socialist Party. Members of the OCI worked closely with Francois Mitterrand as the SP was developed, on a thoroughly opportunist basis, into an instrument of his electoral ambitions. One of the OCI members, Lionel Jospin, became a political aide to Mitterrand, advanced within the hierarchy of the Socialist Party, and eventually attained the office of Prime Minister. It is impossible to determine, retrospectively, whether an open political struggle by the SLL might have arrested the opportunist degeneration of the OCI and its transformation into an instrument of the French state. But such a struggle would have clarified the political issues and alerted the SLL to the dangers posed by opportunist tendencies within its own ranks.

The Founding of the Workers Revolutionary Party and the World Crisis of 1973-75

155. The transformation of the SLL into the Workers Revolutionary Party in November 1973 was not prepared on the basis of a review of the strategic experiences of the international Trotskyist movement. Rather, it was a tactical response to the working class movement against the government of Tory Prime Minister Edward Heath. The International Committee was excluded by the SLL from participating in the discussions that attended the founding of the Workers Revolutionary Party. After the founding congress, the growth of the WRP during this period of working class militancy, which resulted in the fall of the Heath government and the coming to power of a Labour government in March 1974, concealed briefly the mounting problems within the organization.

156. The defeat of the Heath government was one episode in an economic and political crisis that convulsed world capitalism in the period between 1973 and 1975. The end of dollar-gold convertibility unleashed an

inflationary cycle that was exacerbated by a general loss of confidence in the American currency. In October 1973 war broke out in the Middle East, leading to a quadrupling of oil prices by OPEC, which, in turn, triggered the worst recession since the Great Depression of the 1930s. In April 1974 the fascist dictatorship of Salazar in Portugal, which had been in power for nearly a half-century, collapsed beneath the pressure of anti-colonial insurgencies in Africa (Angola and Mozambique) and mounting domestic crises. The first legal May Day was celebrated in Lisbon with a demonstration of several million people. In July 1974 the military junta in Greece, which had seized power in 1967, fell in the wake of a disastrous intervention in Cyprus. In August 1974, President Richard Nixon was forced to resign after the House Judiciary Committee voted for Articles of Impeachment as a result of revelations relating to the Watergate scandal and to illegal military actions that had been ordered by the Administration in Cambodia. Finally, in April 1975, Vietnamese liberation forces entered Saigon, achieved the unification of their country, and brought the neo-colonialist operations of the United States in Indochina to a humiliating conclusion.

Wohlforth's Break with the Workers League

157. The world capitalist crisis and the escalation of class conflict brought to the surface political problems in the Workers League. The growth of the League in the late 1960s and early 1970s had been based to a great extent on the radicalization of student and minority youth. But the political climate on university campuses substantially changed as the withdrawal of US troops from Vietnam began and the draft was ended. The Workers League was confronted with the challenge of turning to the working class. This required not only expanded practical activities, but also a comprehensive Marxist analysis of the objective situation and the assimilation, by a relatively inexperienced party cadre, of the lessons of the ICFI's struggle against Pabloite revisionism. Instead, the work of the party assumed, under Wohlforth's direction, a largely activist character, without a clear political perspective. Wohlforth's political and personal behavior exhibited disturbing signs of disorientation. Egged on by a new personal companion, Nancy Fields, Wohlforth's interventions in the party assumed a frenzied, unprincipled and destructive charac-

ter. Within the space of one year, 1973-74, the Workers League lost more than one-half of its membership.

158. The crisis in the Workers League came to a head in late August 1974. The International Committee learned that Nancy Fields—who, without any experience or qualifications, had been elevated into the leadership by Wohlforth and had become his inseparable companion—had close family connections with high-ranking personnel in the Central Intelligence Agency. It then emerged that Wohlforth, though aware of these family relations, had concealed this information from all other members of the Workers League Central Committee. Nor had Wohlforth informed the International Committee of Nancy Field's background, even though he personally selected her to accompany him to an ICFI conference in May 1974. Several delegates attending that conference came from countries with repressive regimes, which required that political work be carried out in conditions of illegality. The Workers League Central Committee voted to remove Wohlforth as national secretary and, pending an investigation into her background, suspend Fields from membership.[95] One month later, Wohlforth resigned from the Workers League. Soon thereafter, he publicly denounced the International Committee and—repudiating all that he had written over the previous 14 years—rejoined the Socialist Workers Party. Eventually, Wohlforth would abandon socialist politics entirely, denounce the Trotskyist movement as a "cult," and, in the late 1990s, call for American military action in the Balkans (in an article entitled "Give War a Chance").

The Workers League After Wohlforth

159. The political desertion of Wohlforth marked a decisive turning point in the development of the Workers League as a Trotskyist organi-

---

95 The report issued by the ICFI stated that "from the age of 12 until the completion of her university education, Nancy Fields was brought up, educated and financially supported by her aunt and uncle, Albert and Gigs Morris. Albert Morris is head of the CIA's computer operation in Washington as well as being a large stockholder in IBM. He was a member of the OSS, forerunner of the CIA, and worked in Poland as an agent of imperialism. During the 1960s, a frequent house guest at their home in Maine was Richard Helms, ex-director of the CIA and now US Ambassador in Iran." [*Documents of Security and the Fourth International* (New York: Labor Publications, 1985), p. 15.]

zation. Wohlforth's resignation and subsequent repudiation of his own political history expressed not only personal weaknesses. It epitomized specific traits of American petty-bourgeois radicalism—in particular, its contempt for theoretical consistency and a pragmatic disdain for history. The Workers League recognized that the crisis through which it had passed in 1973-74 required more than a criticism of Wohlforth's errors. Thus, in response to Wohlforth's resignation and his denunciation of the ICFI, the Workers League initiated an extensive review of the history of the Fourth International. It was precisely the emphasis on the historical experience of the Trotskyist movement, within the context of the objective development of world capitalism and the international class struggle, that emerged as the essential and distinctive characteristic of the Workers League. The development of Marxist perspective and the strategic orientation to the working class, it repeatedly stressed, was only possible to the extent that the full weight of the historical experience of the Marxist movement was brought to bear in the analysis of contemporary socio-economic processes. In its perspective resolution of November 1978, the Workers League stated:

> The foundation for revolutionary practice, the indispensable basis for any real orientation to the working class from the standpoint of the struggle for power, is the thorough assimilation of the entire body of historical experiences through which the International Committee has passed since 1953. The training of Trotskyist cadre is only possible in the struggle to base every aspect and detail of the party's political work on the historical conquests of the International Committee, derived from the battle against revisionism.[96]

160. The document explained the relationship between this conscious and continuous reworking of the historical experience of the Trotskyist movement and both the theoretical struggle against pragmatism and the practical orientation of the party to the working class:

---

96 *The World Economic-Political Crisis of Capitalism and the Death Agony of US Imperialism* (New York: Labor Publications, 1979), p. 30.

There can be no real turn to the working class outside of the conscious struggle to preserve the lines of historical continuity between the present struggles of the working class and the revolutionary party as a unity of opposites and the whole content of the objective historical experiences of the class and the development of Bolshevism. It is only from the standpoint of the struggle to base the whole work of the Party on the historical gains of the struggle against revisionism, and the immense political and theoretical capital that is the heritage left behind by Trotsky to the Fourth International, that the fight against pragmatism within the ranks of the Party and, therefore, in the working class itself, can be seriously mounted. As soon as the struggle against pragmatism is detached from the fight to maintain the direct historical connections between the daily practice of the cadres and the whole body of historical experiences through which the Trotskyist movement has passed, it degenerates into the most impotent forms of verbal jousting. Or, to put it more accurately, it becomes simply another variety of pragmatism itself.[97]

The Origins of the "Security and the Fourth International" Investigation

161. The intersection of history and politics found expression in the circumstances surrounding Wohlforth's desertion from the Workers League. Although he had initially acknowledged that his failure to inform either the leadership of the Workers League or the International Committee of Fields's family connections was a serious breach of the movement's security, Wohlforth—once he had left the Workers League—declared that the concerns raised by the party were without the slightest justification. Gerry Healy's preoccupation with the issue of security, declared Wohlforth, was evidence of "madness." Joseph Hansen, the principal political leader of the Socialist Workers Party and editor of the Pabloite journal, *Intercontinental Press*, came to Wohlforth's aid with a vitriolic denunciation of Healy. "Wohlforth describes Healy's performance as 'madness,'" Hansen wrote.

---

97 Ibid., p. 36.

"Would it not be preferable and more precise, to use a modern term like 'paranoia'?"[98]

162. Hansen's intervention in support of Wohlforth, aimed at belittling the need for security in the revolutionary socialist movement and discrediting those who took this matter seriously, raised questions of the greatest political and historical significance:

i. Hansen's defense of Wohlforth's negligent attitude toward the security of his own organization came at a time when, in the aftermath of Nixon's resignation, an enormous amount of evidence was emerging about massive government spying on radical and socialist organizations. Hansen's own organization had been the target of a spying operation that spanned nearly 15 years. Documents relating to the so-called COINTELPRO operation, set up by the Federal Bureau of Investigation under the aegis of J. Edgar Hoover, revealed that between 1961 and 1975 the SWP had been flooded with police agents and informants.

ii. The Trotskyist movement had been dealt devastating blows through the infiltration of the Fourth International by agents of the Soviet Union and the United States. The assassination of a significant section of the leadership of the Fourth International between 1937 and 1940 was prepared and executed by Stalinist agents who had penetrated the movement.

iii. Hansen, who libeled Healy's concern for the security of the international Trotskyist movement as "paranoia," had witnessed the assassination of Leon Trotsky by Mercader. It was none other than Hansen who authorized the admission of the GPU agent into Trotsky's villa in Coyoacan on the day of the murder. Hansen also knew that Mercader had developed a personal relationship with a young member of the SWP as a ploy to gain access to Trotsky. James P. Cannon, after Trotsky's assassination, indicted the "carelessness" that had compromised Trotsky's personal security. "We haven't probed deeply enough into the past of people even in leading positions—where they came from, how they live, whom they are

98 "The Secret of Healy's Dialectics," *Intercontinental Press*, March 31, 1975.

married to, etc. Whenever in the past such questions—elementary for a revolutionary organization—were raised, the petty-bourgeois opposition would cry, 'My God, you are invading the private lives of comrades!' Yes, that is precisely what we were doing, or more correctly, threatening to do—nothing ever came of it in the past. If we had checked up on such matters a little more carefully we might have prevented some bad things in the days gone by."[99]

163. Given this context, Hansen's attack on Healy was not only scurrilous. It was nothing less than an attempt to disarm the cadre of the Trotskyist movement in the face of real threats from the capitalist state and its agencies. The International Committee decided that the most appropriate answer to Hansen and Wohlforth would be to review the historical experience of the Fourth International in relation to problems of security. Specifically, this entailed an investigation into the events leading up to the assassination of Trotsky. At its Sixth Congress in May 1975, the ICFI voted to initiate this investigation, whose results were to be published until the title, "Security and the Fourth International."

The Role of Joseph Hansen

164. The initial stages of the investigation uncovered recently declassified documents, which revealed the conspiracy that prepared Trotsky's assassination and the fatal role played by agents who had managed to infiltrate all the major political centers of the Fourth International. The ICFI uncovered documents relating to the activities of agents such as Mark Zborowski, who became the principal assistant of Trotsky's son, Leon Sedov. Zborowski played a key role in the murder of Sedov and other leading members of the Fourth International in Europe. Another important Stalinist agent, who supplied the Kremlin with valuable information on Trotsky's activities was Sylvia Caldwell (née Callen), the personal secretary of James P. Cannon. But the most significant informa-

---

99 James P. Cannon, *The Socialist Workers Party in World War II: Writings and Speeches, 1940-43* [New York: Pathfinder Press, 1975], pp. 81-82.

tion uncovered by the ICFI related to the activities of Joseph Hansen. Documents discovered in the US National Archives, and others obtained through the Freedom of Information Act, revealed that Hansen, immediately after the assassination of Trotsky, sought out and established a covert relationship with high-level US government agents. One such document, a letter from the American Consul in Mexico City to an official in the State Department, dated September 25, 1940, reported that Hansen "wishes to be put in touch with someone in your confidence located in New York to whom confidential information could be imparted with impunity."[100]

165. The ICFI discovered conclusive evidence that Joseph Hansen had functioned as an agent inside the Trotskyist movement. A lawsuit brought by Alan Gelfand against the US government, alleging state control of the Socialist Workers Party, forced the release of official documents that substantiated the findings of the Security and the Fourth International investigation. Among the most significant facts uncovered as a result of the lawsuit was that the FBI had known, from at least the mid-1940s, that Joseph Hansen had worked for the GPU inside the SWP. He had been identified as a Stalinist agent by former Communist Party leader Louis Budenz, the same man who had publicly exposed Sylvia Caldwell. This revelation made clear why Hansen and the SWP leadership vehemently denounced Budenz and defended Caldwell. To admit the truth of Budenz's allegations against Caldwell would lend substantial credibility to his identification of Hansen as an agent. Thus, up until the court-ordered release of Sylvia Caldwell's grand jury testimony, in which she admitted to having worked inside the SWP as a GPU spy, the SWP defended her as an "exemplary" comrade. Reba Hansen, the wife of Joseph Hansen, lied publicly about the reasons for Caldwell's sudden departure from the party in 1947 (the year Budenz's revelations were made public). Describing Caldwell as "a warm human being," Reba Hansen claimed that "Sylvia left New York in 1947 because of family obligations."[101] SWP national secretary Jack Barnes, in testimony given during the trial of Gelfand's lawsuit, declared that Caldwell "is one of

---

100   *Documents of Security and the Fourth International*, p. 115.

101   *James P. Cannon As We Knew Him* (New York: Pathfinder Press, 1976), p. 233.

my heroes after the harassment and what she's been through in the last couple of years."[102]

A Phony "Verdict":
The Pabloites Endorse the Cover-up of Stalinist Crimes

166. Despite the evidence uncovered by the ICFI, all the opportunist and Pabloite organizations opposed the Security and the Fourth International investigation. In September 1976, virtually every leading figure in the Pabloite movement issued a so-called "Verdict" denouncing Security and the Fourth International as a "Shameless Frame-up." Depositions taken by Gelfand of SWP officials responsible for the publication of the "Verdict" established that none of its signatories had reviewed any of the evidence gathered by the ICFI before affixing their names to the denunciation of "Security and the Fourth International." Repeated calls by the International Committee for the establishment of a commission of inquiry to examine the evidence went unanswered. Political interests played a decisive role in the Pabloites' response. They had no interest in revisiting the issue of Trotsky's assassination and bringing to the attention of a new generation of workers the history of Stalinist crimes. Nor did they object when the SWP went into court in 1982 in support of GPU murderer Mark Zborowski's efforts to quash a subpoena obtained by Gelfand, compelling Zborowski to answer questions relating to the infiltration of the Socialist Workers Party. Zborowski, who was living in comfortable retirement in San Francisco, challenged the subpoena on the grounds that testimony contributing to the exposure of agents inside the SWP would constitute a violation of the recently passed Intelligence Identities Protection Act. The court upheld Zborowski's appeal.

167.   In the quarter century that has passed since the completion of the Security and the Fourth International investigation, many of its findings have been substantiated by the release of official Soviet documents. The so-called "Venona Papers"—decrypted files from Soviet intelligence sources—have definitively identified not only Caldwell, but also Robert

---

102   *The Gelfand Case*, Volume II (New York: Labor Publications, 1985) p. 635.

Sheldon Harte—an SWP member sent down to Mexico to serve as a guard—as a Stalinist agent. When the ICFI initially published information incriminating Harte, this, too, was denounced by the SWP and the Pabloites as a slander. The validation of the charges made by the ICFI has produced no retraction by any of the Pabloite organizations of their denunciations of Security and the Fourth International.

168. Another peculiar set of facts emerged as a byproduct of the Security investigation. Virtually the entire central leadership of the Socialist Workers Party—including a majority of its political committee—had attended Carleton College, a small liberal arts school in the Midwest. There was no record that the SWP had conducted any systematic work on the Carleton campus during the period between 1960 and 1964, when so many of its students, including Jack Barnes, entered the party and were rapidly promoted into its leadership. The medium of their transformation from conservative Midwestern students (Jack Barnes had been a Republican) into leaders of an ostensibly revolutionary organization was the Fair Play for Cuba Committee, which was manipulated by, and riddled with, FBI agents. No credible explanation has been provided by the SWP leadership for the Carleton College phenomenon.

169. As the International Committee's investigation uncovered evermore incriminating evidence implicating Hansen as an agent, the counter-campaign of the SWP and the Pabloites assumed an increasingly provocative character. On January 14, 1977, the Pabloites held in London a public meeting of their supporters to denounce Security and the Fourth International and, in particular, Gerry Healy. Among those addressing the assembly were Ernest Mandel, Tariq Ali (leader of the British Pabloite organization), Pierre Lambert (leader of the OCI), and Tim Wohlforth. Prior to the meeting, the Workers Revolutionary Party sent a letter addressed to the leaders of the Pabloite organizations, calling for the establishment of a parity commission, consisting of an equal number of members from the ICFI and United Secretariat, to examine the evidence that had been uncovered by the investigation. The letter was not answered, nor was it acknowledged at the January 14 meeting. Instead, the meeting was given over entirely to vituperative denunciations of Healy. When Healy rose from the audience to request that he be given an opportunity to respond to the attacks, he was refused.

170. Despite the Pabloite stonewalling, the investigation continued. In May 1977, the ICFI located Sylvia Caldwell in a suburb outside Chicago, living without a fixed address in a trailer park. She had, since leaving the SWP, remarried (her first husband, Stalinist agent Zalmond Franklin, had died in 1958), and was now Sylvia Doxsee. She claimed to have no recollection of having been a member of the SWP, while at the same time declaring that James P. Cannon was a man of no particular importance. The ICFI published photos of Doxsee and portions of the transcript of its interview with her in June 1977. The SWP responded to this with a public campaign that sought to label the Workers League as a "violent" organization. This campaign was spearheaded by Hansen himself who, while warning that the investigation would have "deadly consequences" for the International Committee, wrote that "the Healyites are quite capable of initiating physical violence against other sectors of the labor movement... "[103] It had long been the modus operandi of the Stalinists to denounce the Trotskyist movement as "violent" even as they prepared physical attacks against it. Four months later, on October 16, 1977, Tom Henehan, a leading member of the Workers League, was shot in New York City while supervising a public function of its youth organization, the Young Socialists. He died of his wounds in hospital, just a few hours later. Henehan's murder had all the characteristics of a professional assassination, carried out by skilled gunmen, who entered the premises where the function was being held and, without any cause, fired on Henehan. The New York City press immediately labeled the assault a "senseless killing," and the police refused to conduct any investigation. Though the two killers had been identified by eyewitnesses, no attempt was made by the police to apprehend them. The police inaction was abetted by the Pabloites, who refused to either report or denounce the murder of Tom Henehan. The Workers League conducted an independent political campaign to mobilize public support behind the demand for the apprehension of the assassins. In the course of this campaign tens of thousands of workers, and the representatives of trade union organizations representing several million workers, signed petitions endorsing the Workers League's demand. Finally, in October 1980, the police acceded to this public pressure and arrested the killers, Angelo

---

103 *Intercontinental Press,* June 20, 1977.

Torres and Edwin Sequinot. Their trial was held in July 1981. They were found guilty and sentenced to lengthy prison terms. However, the defendants did not testify and they provided no explanation for their actions.

A Shift in the World Situation: The Capitalist Counter-Offensive

171. The period between 1968 and 1975 witnessed an immense upsurge of the working class. Left-wing and socialist movements grew significantly throughout the world. In the midst of a powerful strike movement of British workers in the summer of 1972, the *Daily Telegraph* published an editorial headlined, "Who Shall Rule?," raising openly the specter of a revolutionary overturn of the capitalist state by the working class. In the United States, the attempt by the Nixon administration—with the support of the AFL-CIO bureaucracy—to impose wage controls failed in the face of widespread defiance by an increasingly militant working class. In country after country, the workers demonstrated a determination to fight in defense of their class interests. But the central historical problem identified by Leon Trotsky in 1938—the "historical crisis of the leadership of the proletariat"—remained unsolved. The old Stalinist and Social-Democratic labor and trade union bureaucracies utilized their positions of influence, with the critical assistance of the Pabloite tendencies, to divert, disorient and suppress mass struggles that threatened bourgeois rule. Situations with immense revolutionary potential were misdirected, defused, betrayed and led to defeat. The consequences of the political treachery of the Stalinists and Social Democrats found their most terrible expression in Chile, where the "socialist" Allende government, abetted by the Communist Party, did everything it possibly could to prevent the working class from taking power. That Allende himself lost his life as a consequence of his efforts to prevent the overthrow of the bourgeois state does not lessen his responsibility for facilitating the military coup, led by General Augusto Pinochet, of September 11, 1973.

172. The inability of the working class to break through the log-jam created by its own organizations provided the bourgeoisie with the time it needed to stabilize and reorganize the fragile world order. By mid-1975 there were signs that the worst of the economic crisis had passed. Dollars that had

flowed into the Middle East after the quadrupling of oil prices ("petro-dollars") were recycled by the International Monetary Fund back to the major capitalist banking centers, to provide new liquidity for the world financial system. The IMF-sponsored "reflation" provided Britain's Labour Party prime minister, Harold Wilson, with the financial credits he needed to arrange temporary compromises with the trade union bureaucracy, while preparing the ground for renewed attacks on the working class. The reactionary political intentions of the Labour government found their most conscious expression in September 1975, when Wilson's government ordered an unprecedented police raid on the education center of the Workers Revolutionary Party.

173.   By late 1975 the international bourgeoisie was able to begin exploiting the social frustrations produced by the inability of the working class to implement a revolutionary socialist solution to the crisis. In Australia, in November 1975, Governor-General Sir John Kerr intervened in the political crisis created by the provocative actions of the bourgeois Liberal Party to remove from power the democratically-elected Labor government of Gough Whitlam. This action took place at a time when it was well known that the CIA was heavily engaged in efforts to destabilize the Whitlam government. Kerr's "coup" was met by massive protests by the working class, demanding that Whitlam stand his ground and openly defy Kerr. The call for Whitlam to "sack" Kerr was voiced by hundreds of thousands of working class protestors throughout Australia. Instead, Whitlam capitulated cravenly to the Governor-General and left office. Such exhibitions of political cowardice by the labor bureaucracies served only to encourage the international bourgeoisie to believe that it could attack the working class with impunity. In Argentina, the military overthrew the Peronist regime—which had been backed by the Pabloites—and initiated a reign of terror against the left. In Sri Lanka and Israel, right-wing governments came to power, espousing the anti-Keynesian monetarism promoted by Milton Friedman, whose economic theories had already been set to work by the Chilean dictatorship.

174.   In May 1979 the Tory party, led by Margaret Thatcher, came to power in Britain. The political conditions for her victory were created by the right-wing policies of the Labour government. Working class anger erupted in a wave of strikes in late 1978 and early 1979, the so-called "Winter of Discontent." All of these struggles were sabotaged by the trade

union bureaucracy. In the United States, the Carter administration shifted sharply to the right in the wake of a protracted miners' strike in 1977-78 that lasted more than 100 days. The government's invocation of the Taft-Hartley Act, ordering the miners back to work, was ignored by the strikers and could not be enforced. The American ruling class decided that further attacks on the working class required more careful preparation. In August 1979 President Carter appointed Paul Volcker chairman of the Federal Reserve. Volcker proceeded to raise interest rates to unprecedented levels, with the intention of provoking a recession that would significantly raise unemployment levels, weaken the working class, and prepare the ground for a major right-wing offensive. The sharp turn toward class confrontation was confirmed with the Republican Party's nomination of Ronald Reagan and his election as president in November 1980. Reagan was inaugurated in January 1981. Little more than six months later, in August, the Reagan administration responded to the strike called by the Professional Air Traffic Controllers Organization (PATCO) by firing 11,000 striking controllers. The AFL-CIO refused to take any action to defend the workers. This attack marked the beginning of the end of the trade union movement as a significant social force in the United States. A green light had been given by the government to the corporations, authorizing open strike breaking. The AFL-CIO, moreover, made it very clear that it would do nothing to stop the right-wing rampage against the working class.

175.   The setbacks suffered by the working class in the major centers of capitalism cleared the way for a more aggressive assertion of imperialist interests. Prime Minister Thatcher dispatched the British navy to the South Atlantic to dislodge Argentina from the Malvinas (Falkland Islands). The Reagan administration became deeply entangled in a dirty war against left-wing forces in El Salvador and Nicaragua, intensified its collaboration with the mujahedeen in Afghanistan, sent US forces into Lebanon, escalated its anti-Soviet "Evil Empire" rhetoric, and dispatched troops to Grenada.

The Crisis in the Workers Revolutionary Party

176.   Contrary to the expectations of the Workers Revolutionary Party, the return of the Labourites to power in England in March 1974 did not

quickly lead to confrontations between the working class and the new government. The IMF-backed reflation provided maneuvering room for the Labour government. This new situation revealed the weaknesses in the political foundations of the WRP. Because the conversion of the Socialist Labour League into the WRP, and the "mass recruitment" campaigns that had accompanied it, had been based mainly on appeals to widespread and elementary anti-Tory sentiment in the working class, the new party and its membership were ill-equipped to deal with the more complex situation created by the return of the Labourites to power.

177. The WRP sought to counteract the difficulties it faced in the development of the working class by seeking a base of support elsewhere. The cultivation of relations, beginning in 1976, with various national liberation movements and bourgeois nationalist regimes in the Middle East expressed a high degree of political disorientation. As the WRP retreated from its earlier insistence on the centrality of the struggle against revisionism in the building of the Marxist movement, Healy and his closest associates, Cliff Slaughter and Michael Banda, drifted more and more openly toward the Pabloite conceptions they had fought in the 1950s and 1960s. Their capitulation to the Pabloite program was accompanied by the development of an idealist mystification of Marxism that grossly distorted the dialectical materialist method of analysis.

The Workers League's Critique of the WRP

178. In the 1960s and early 1970s the British Trotskyist movement had exerted an extremely positive influence on the Workers League. The emergence and early development of the Workers League would not have been possible without the invaluable experience of the Socialist Labour League and Gerry Healy. And yet, particularly in the aftermath of the break with Wohlforth, the development of the Workers League proceeded in a manner that was notably different from that of the Workers Revolutionary Party. The central difference consisted in the attention paid by the Workers League to the history of the Trotskyist movement and the lessons of the struggle against Pabloism.

179. In the aftermath of the break with Wohlforth, the Workers League oriented its work strongly toward the working class. Beginning in the 1970s, it developed a substantial presence in the struggles of the most militant sections, most notably among the coal miners of the UMWA. In 1978 the Workers League decided to relocate its political center in Detroit. The purpose of this relocation was to establish a closer link between the party and the daily life and struggles of the working class. In the years that followed, the Workers League and its newspaper, *The Bulletin*, played a significant role in the strikes of the air traffic controllers, Phelps Dodge Copper miners, Greyhound drivers, Hormel workers, and numerous strikes in the coal fields of West Virginia and Kentucky. And yet all these struggles were seen, not as occasions for the celebration of trade union militancy, but as essentially political struggles that required the development of socialist consciousness and Marxist leadership within the working class. This work made the Workers League all the more conscious of the importance of a clearly worked out and comprehensive international revolutionary strategy.

180. The differences between the WRP and the Workers League emerged openly in the autumn of 1982. In an essay published to commemorate the fifth anniversary of the murder of Tom Henehan, David North, national secretary of the Workers League, stressed the significance of history in the education of the cadre of the Marxist movement. He wrote:

> The real heart of cadre training is the conscious subordination of all who join the Party to the revolutionary principles through which the historical continuity of the Marxist movement is expressed. By 'historical continuity,' we have in mind the unbroken chain of political and ideological struggle by our international movement against Stalinism, Social Democracy, revisionism and all other enemies of the working class…
>
> Revisionists and political charlatans of all descriptions invariably base their politics and policies on the immediate and practical needs of the hour. Principled considerations, i.e., those which arise out of a serious study of the history of the international workers' movement, knowledge of its development as a law-governed process, and, flowing from that, a constant critical reworking of its objective experiences, are utterly foreign to these pragmatists…

A leadership which does not strive collectively to assimilate the whole of this history cannot adequately fulfill its revolutionary responsibilities to the working class. Without a real knowledge of the historical development of the Trotskyist movement, references to dialectical materialism are not merely hollow; such empty references pave the way for a real distortion of the dialectical method. The source of theory lies not in thought but in the objective world. Thus the development of Trotskyism proceeds from the fresh experiences of the class struggle, which are posited on the entire historically-derived knowledge of our movement.[104]

181. North submitted to the Workers Revolutionary Party a detailed critique of a pamphlet written by Healy, *Studies in Dialectical Materialism*. This critique established that Healy's conception of dialectics involved a repudiation of materialism and a reversion to the type of subjective idealist philosophy that Marx had overcome in his critique of the Left Hegelians in the early 1840s. North wrote:

> Cde. Healy's *Studies in Dialectical Materialism* suffers from one decisive defect: they essentially ignore the achievements of both Marx and Lenin in the materialist reworking of the Hegelian dialectic. Thus, Hegel is approached uncritically, essentially in the manner of the Left Hegelians against whom Marx struggled. ...
>
> Cde. Healy does not take into account the oft-repeated warnings of both Marx and Engels that the Hegelian dialectic was unusable in the form it was left behind. Thus, Cde. Healy seeks to explain the process of cognition directly from the Hegelian Logic. This is a false approach. The process of thought cannot be explained from the Logic any more than the nature of the State could be explained from the Logic. ...
>
> The phrase "standing Hegel on his feet" should not be used to diminish the profound scientific achievement embodied in this task. What was involved was nothing less than the establishment of the

---

104   David North, *Leon Trotsky and the Development of Marxism* (Detroit, 1985) pp. 5; 17-18.

materialist world scientific outlook through which laws of nature, society and consciousness are cognized. The chief concern of philosophy was no longer the "matter of Logic" but the "logic of the matter."

Marx clearly revealed that the Hegelian logical schema, when utilized as given, leads inevitably to sophistry, via the manipulation of logical categories and the further manipulation of empirical facts to fit the pre-existing categories.[105]

182. In his conclusion, North summarized his critique of the political evolution of the ICFI under the leadership of the WRP. "*Studies in Dialectics*", North wrote, "has brought into the open a crisis that has been developing within the International Committee for a considerable period of time. For several years (in my opinion, this began in 1976 and only began to predominate in 1978), in the name of the struggle for dialectical materialism and against propagandism, the International Committee has drifted steadily away from a struggle for Trotskyism." The critique of Healy's theoretical method was linked to an analysis of the WRP's relations with bourgeois national regimes in the Middle East. "A vulgarization of Marxism, palmed off as the 'struggle for dialectics,' has been accompanied by an unmistakable opportunist drift within the International Committee, especially in the WRP," North wrote. "Marxist defense of national liberation movements and the struggle against imperialism has been interpreted in an opportunist fashion of uncritical support for various bourgeois nationalist regimes."[106]

183. The Workers League presented a more comprehensive analysis of the degeneration of the WRP in January-February 1984. In a letter dated January 23, 1984 to Michael Banda, the general secretary of the WRP, North stated that the Workers League had become "deeply troubled by the growing signs of a political drift toward political positions quite similar—both in conclusions and methodology—to those we have historically associated with Pabloism." He pointed out that the International Committee:

---

105   *Fourth International* (Detroit, 1986), Volume 13, No. 2, Autumn 1986, pp. 16-18.

106   Ibid., p. 23.

...has for some time been working without a clear and politically-unified perspective to guide its practice. Rather than a perspective for the building of sections of the International Committee in every country, the central focus of the IC's work for several years has been the development of alliances with various bourgeois nationalist regimes and liberation movements. The content of these alliances has less and less reflected any clear orientation toward the development of our own forces as central to the fight to establish the leading role of the proletariat in the anti-imperialist struggle in the semi-colonial countries. The very conceptions advanced by the SWP in relation to Cuba and Algeria, which we attacked so vigorously in the early 1960s, appear with increasing frequency within our own press.[107]

184. North amplified the Workers League's criticism in a report to the ICFI on February 11, 1984, which placed the adaptation of the WRP to bourgeois nationalism within the context of the IC's decades-long struggle against Pabloism, while also pointing to the WRP's opportunist relations with reformist tendencies in Britain. North explained:

> The International Committee is based upon the traditions and principles established through the political, theoretical and organizational struggles of all previous generations of Marxists—and the way in which this continuity of the IC with these previous generations has developed is through the struggle against every variety of anti-Marxism that has emerged within the workers' movement, especially within the Trotskyist movement itself.[108]

185. North noted that the US SWP's explicit repudiation of the Theory of Permanent Revolution—proclaimed by Barnes in late 1982 —vindicated the ICFI's fight against Pabloite revisionism. In place of the struggle for the political independence of the working class, the SWP promoted bourgeois nationalist and petty-bourgeois movements such as the New Jewel movement in Grenada, the Sandinistas in

---

107   Ibid., p. 35.

108   Ibid., p. 39.

Nicaragua, and the Farabundo Marti of El Salvador. Within this context, North stressed the need to examine the political experiences of the ICFI. Noting its relations with national movements in the Middle East, North stated:

> It is clear that by mid-1978 a general orientation toward relations with nationalist regimes and liberation movements was developing without any corresponding perspective for the actual building of our own forces inside the working class. An entirely uncritical and incorrect appraisal began to emerge ever more openly within our press, inviting the cadres and the working class to view these bourgeois nationalists as "anti-imperialist" leaders to whom political support must be given.[109]

186. North criticized the WRP's support for Saddam Hussein's repression of the Iraqi Communist Party, including the execution of 21 members in 1979; the praise given to the Iranian regime of Ayatollah Khomeini after an initially correct appraisal of the February 1979 revolution; and the uncritical support for the leader of the Libyan Jamahiriya, Muammar al-Gadafi, between 1977 and 1983. North also cited the relations that the WRP had established with sections of the Labour Party, including Ken Livingstone and Ted Knight, and the Greater London Council.

187. The Workers Revolutionary Party refused to engage in a discussion of these differences. Instead, it issued threats to sever relations with the Workers League if it persisted in its criticisms. This unprincipled and opportunist course had, ultimately, devastating consequences for the WRP. Within little more than one year, in the autumn of 1985, the WRP was shattered by an organizational crisis that was the outcome of more than a decade of political retreat from the principles upon which the founding of the Fourth International and the International Committee had been based. Its refusal to accept the political counsel of the ICFI, and its pursuit of political interests that were conceived of in entirely nationalist terms, led to the split of February 1986.

---

109 Ibid., pp. 42-43.

The Collapse of the WRP and the Split in the International Committee

188.   In August 1985, members of the International Committee were summoned to London, where they were informed by Healy and other leaders of the WRP that the British section was confronted with a serious financial crisis. The ICFI members were told that the problems were caused by unexpected tax surcharges and a substantial increase in the cost of distributing the WRP's daily newspaper, the *Newsline*. An urgent appeal was made by the WRP leaders for financial assistance from the ICFI sections. As was soon to emerge, the report given to the ICFI consisted almost entirely of lies. Moreover, the WRP did not inform the IC members that a crisis had erupted in the leadership of the British section over allegations of improper personal conduct by Healy himself. Demands raised within the Central Committee for a control commission investigation of these allegations were being opposed, not only by Healy, but also by Michael Banda and Cliff Slaughter. While seeking money from the ICFI to shore up the problems created by the internal political crisis in the British section, the WRP sought to conceal these facts from the ICFI members. However, as the factional conflict within the WRP intensified over the next few weeks, the facts of the crisis became known to the ICFI. David North, representing the Workers League, Nick Beams (from the Socialist Labour League in Australia), Ulrich Rippert and Peter Schwarz (from the Bund Sozialistischer Arbeiter in Germany), and Keerthi Balasuriya (from the Revolutionary Communist League in Sri Lanka) traveled to Britain to review the political situation in the Workers Revolutionary Party. They insisted that the crisis that had developed inside the British section was rooted in long-standing political issues relating to international program and perspectives. They informed the WRP leaders that the ICFI would not take sides in the struggle among different unprincipled factions in the WRP leadership. The ICFI rejected entirely the efforts of WRP leaders to utilize the international movement for their own nationalist and opportunist purposes. Indeed, the political recovery of the WRP from its crisis was possible only to the extent that the British organization accepted the discipline of the international movement.

189. On October 25, 1985, after examining the allegations against Healy, the International Committee voted for his expulsion. The statement issued by the ICFI declared:

> In expelling Healy the ICFI has no intention of denying the political contributions which he made in the past, particularly in the struggle against Pabloite revisionism in the 1950s and the 1960s.
>
> In fact, this expulsion is the end product of his rejection of the Trotskyist principles upon which these past struggles were based and his descent into the most vulgar forms of opportunism.
>
> The political and personal degeneration of Healy can be clearly traced to his ever more explicit separation of the practical and organizational gains of the Trotskyist movement in Britain from the historically and internationally grounded struggles against Stalinism and revisionism from which these achievements arose.
>
> The increasing subordination of questions of principle to immediate practical needs centered on securing the growth of the Party apparatus, degenerating into political opportunism which steadily eroded his own political and moral defenses against the pressures of imperialism in the oldest capitalist country in the world.
>
> Under these conditions his serious subjective weaknesses played an increasingly dangerous political role.
>
> Acting ever more arbitrarily within both the WRP and the ICFI, Healy increasingly attributed the advances of the World Party not to the Marxist principles of the Fourth International and to the collective struggle of its cadre, but rather to his own personal abilities.
>
> His self-glorification of his intuitive judgments led inevitably to a gross vulgarization of materialist dialectics and Healy's transformation into a thoroughgoing subjective idealist and pragmatist.
>
> In place of his past interest in the complex problems of developing the cadre of the international Trotskyist movement, Healy's practice became almost entirely preoccupied with developing unprincipled relations with bourgeois nationalist leaders and with trade union and Labour Party reformists in Britain.
>
> His personal life-style underwent a corresponding degeneration.

Those like Healy, who abandon the principles on which they once fought and who refuse to subordinate themselves to the ICFI in the building of its national sections, must inevitably degenerate under the pressure of the class enemy.

There can be no exception to this historical law.

The ICFI affirms that no leader stands above the historic interests of the working class.[110]

190. Notwithstanding their factional conflict with Healy, Banda and Slaughter shared his opportunist and nationalist perspective. They, no less than Healy, sought to avoid an examination of the origins and development of the crisis of the organization in which they had played a leading role for more than three decades. Moreover, it soon became clear that Banda and Slaughter would not accept international constraints upon the political alliances and activities of the WRP. On December 11, 1985, the Workers League Political Committee wrote to the Central Committee of the WRP:

During the past three months, the Workers League has stated repeatedly that the political crisis within the Workers Revolutionary Party can be overcome only through the closest collaboration of the British section with its international comrades. Unfortunately, after years of systematic miseducation under Healy there are many comrades within the leadership of the WRP who view the International Committee with contempt, and consider appeals of the IC for genuine collaboration and consultation as an unwarranted intrusion into the life of the British section. References to the "subordination of the WRP to the International Committee" evoke a hostile response from some comrades. Of course, we are not dealing with the subjective weaknesses of individual members. The existence of powerful nationalist tendencies within the WRP is a political reflection of the historical development of the working class in the world's oldest imperialist country. Insofar as they are recognized and consciously fought these tendencies can be overcome, and the responsibility

---

110   *Fourth International*, Volume 13, No. 2, Autumn 1986, p. 52.

for waging this struggle falls upon the leadership of the Workers Revolutionary Party.

The great danger that we now confront is that anti-internationalism is being encouraged by the leadership. The national autonomy of the Workers Revolutionary Party is being counterposed to the authority of the International Committee as the leading body of the World Party of Socialist Revolution.[111]

191. In response to Slaughter's assertion that "Internationalism consists precisely of laying down ... class lines and fighting them through," the Political Committee asked:

> But by what process are these "class lines" determined? Does it require the existence of the Fourth International? Comrade Slaughter's definition suggests—and this is the explicit content of his entire letter—that any national organization can rise to the level of internationalism by establishing, on its own, the "class lines and fighting them through." ...

The Workers League reminded Slaughter:

> Those parties which uphold Trotskyism as the contemporary development of Marxist principles and program are organized in the Fourth International and accept the authority of the International Committee. To base one's definition of internationalism on the separation of the program from its organizational expression is to adopt the standpoint of all those revisionist and centrist opponents of Trotskyism who deny the continuity of Marxism, embodied in the ICFI, in order to retain freedom of action within their national theater of operations.[112]

192. On December 16, 1985, the International Committee received a report from an International Control Commission that it had formed to

111   Ibid., p. 77.

112   Ibid.

examine the political and financial relations that had been established by the WRP with various bourgeois national regimes in the Middle East between 1976 and 1985. This report established conclusively that the WRP had entered into political relations that betrayed the principles of the Fourth International, while keeping these relations hidden from the ICFI. The International Committee voted, over objections of WRP delegates representing the Slaughter and Banda factions, to suspend the WRP from membership in the international organization. This resolution was supported by David Hyland, who represented a substantial section of the WRP membership that was in political agreement with the International Committee.

193.   The suspension of the WRP represented an unequivocal assertion of the principles of revolutionary internationalism within the Fourth International. With this action the ICFI made clear that it would not tolerate the subordination of international Trotskyist principles to any form of national opportunism. The purpose of the suspension was not to punish the WRP, but to establish the conditions for membership in the ICFI. A second resolution passed by the ICFI on December 17, 1985 enumerated the historical and programmatic foundations upon which the International Committee was based. It called upon the WRP to reaffirm these principles and, in so doing, prepare for its own rapid readmission into the ICFI. The statement concluded:

> The ICFI and the Central Committee of the WRP shall now work closely together to overcome as quickly as possible the existing problems which are the legacy of the nationalist degeneration of the WRP under Healy, to reassert the basic principles of internationalism within the WRP, and on this basis restore its full membership in the International Committee of the Fourth International. The organizational structure of this relationship shall at all times be based on the Leninist principles of democratic centralism, which are elaborated in the statutes of the Fourth International.[113]

194.   Once again, the WRP delegates, with the exception of David Hyland, voted against this resolution. Their vote made clear that the WRP

---

113   Ibid., p. 102.

did not accept either the program or the authority of the International Committee. One month later, the WRP Central Committee rescinded its previous agreement, made in October 1985, to reregister its membership by admitting into its ranks only those who agreed that membership in the British section required acceptance of the political authority of the International Committee. Hyland and two other members of the WRP Central Committee opposed the WRP's repudiation of this agreement. The WRP Central Committee vote signified a split from the International Committee. On February 8, 1986, the WRP held a rump congress from which all supporters of the International Committee were excluded. This political travesty marked the definitive end of the WRP as a Trotskyist organization. The main document prepared for this congress was an anti-Trotskyist diatribe composed by Banda, entitled *27 Reasons Why the International Committee Should be Buried Forthwith and the Fourth International Built.* Within months of writing this document, Banda repudiated his nearly 40–year association with the Fourth International and proclaimed his admiration for Stalin. As for the WRP, its various factions disintegrated one by one. Within less than a decade, Slaughter and other former leaders of the WRP were heavily involved in the US-NATO operation in Bosnia. The only viable political tendency in the British organization that was to emerge from the collapse of the WRP was that led by Dave Hyland, which upheld the principles of the ICFI. This tendency established the International Communist Party in February 1986, the forerunner to the present-day Socialist Equality Party, the British section of the ICFI.

A Further Comment on
the Cause and Significance of the Split in the ICFI

195.   As in 1953, the split in the International Committee that developed between 1982 and 1986 anticipated enormous changes, which were to shatter, in the last half of the 1980s, the structure of world politics as it had existed in the four decades following the end of World War II. The protracted crisis of the WRP was a complex and contradictory process. Its basic source lay not in the weaknesses of one or another individual, but

in changes in the relationship of class forces on an international scale. It is not uncommon that a political party, which for many decades has played an immensely positive role in the development of the working class, enters into crisis in a later period as new conditions emerge and new tasks are posed. The most tragic examples of this historical phenomenon are the German Social Democracy and the Bolshevik Party. But their historical achievements are not erased by their ultimate fate.

196.   Nor are the achievements of the SLL/WRP and its principal leader, Gerry Healy, obliterated by the later degeneration of the organization. In insisting on an objective appraisal of the history of the SLL/WRP, it is worth recalling advice that Healy gave to Wohlforth in December 1972, after the death of Max Shachtman. Wohlforth had written an obituary of Shachtman in which he denounced, as was appropriate, the deceased's betrayal of socialism and the working class during the final decades of his life. But Wohlforth included in his condemnation the following declaration: "Shachtman died a traitor to his class and a counter-revolutionary. That is the long and short of it." Replying to Wohlforth, Healy noted: "This phrase itself seems at once paradoxical because Shachtman didn't just die, he also lived. Naturally the memory of someone who finally betrayed disgracefully does not give rise to kind feelings. However, we are not here to attribute responsibilities, but to understand."[114]

197.   For many years, particularly after the SWP's return to Pabloism in 1963, the British Trotskyists stood virtually alone in their defense of the program and heritage of the Fourth International. With the OCI an increasingly unreliable ally and, by the late 1960s, a political opponent, the SLL intransigently opposed the efforts of the Pabloites to liquidate the Fourth International into the milieu of Stalinism, bourgeois nationalism and petty-bourgeois radicalism. With little international support, the SLL opposed Pabloite liquidationism by developing, to the best of its abilities, a powerful revolutionary organization in Britain. Into this project Healy threw his extraordinary gifts as a revolutionary organizer and orator. While the Pabloites insisted that Trotskyism had no independent political role to play, the SLL engaged in relentless political warfare against

---

114   *The Fourth International and the Renegade Wohlforth* [*Trotskyism versus Revisionism, Volume Seven*] (Detroit: Labor Publications, 1984), p. 228.

the British Labour Party and captured the political leadership of its youth movement, the Young Socialists. When the British Labourites sought to counter this offensive by proscribing *Keep Left*, the newspaper of the Young Socialists, the SLL and its supporters in the YS fought back and built up a circulation of 10,000 readers. Finally, the Young Socialists became officially the youth movement of the Trotskyist movement in Britain. The Pabloites responded to the advances of the SLL by organizing vicious political witchhunts, enthusiastically backed by the Stalinists, who sought to label the SLL as a "violent" organization.

198.   Given the conditions of political isolation, the SLL came increasingly to see the development of the Fourth International as a by-product of the growth of its organization in England. The successes of the movement in England, it reasoned, would provide the basis for the growth of the International Committee. Thus, over time, the forms and habits of work assumed an increasingly nationalistic coloration. What was, in fact, a temporary relation of political forces—one which imparted to the work in Britain an overwhelming weight within the International Committee— was apotheosized into an increasingly nationalistic conception of the relationship between the SLL/WRP and the Fourth International. The various forms of opportunist practices that were developed by the WRP in the 1970s and into the 1980s were justified by Healy, at least to himself, on the grounds that by "building the party" in England, he was, in the long run, laying the foundations for the international expansion of the ICFI. Even though there had been a substantial political development in the 1970s and early 1980s in different sections of the International Committee, the WRP tended to view the international organization as little more than an adjunct to its own British-based organization.

199.   The essential problem with this approach was that it was based on a nationalistic premise that ran counter to the political traditions of the Fourth International and collided with objective processes of global socio-economic and political development. The crisis of the WRP was part of a broader process that was sweeping through all the mass parties and trade union organizations based historically on the working class. Whatever their differences in organizational structure and political allegiances, the Stalinist, Social-Democratic and reformist organizations were all based on a nationalist program. This essential similarity con-

nected even such apparently irreconcilable enemies as the American AFL-CIO and the Communist Party of the Soviet Union. While the latter's program based itself on the socialist potential of the productive forces of the USSR, the former's reformist aspirations were premised on the supposedly inexhaustible resources and wealth of American capitalism. Both organizations entered into crisis when developments in technology, and the resulting changes in production and the circulation of capital, rendered the national-reformist perspectives of the post-World War II era obsolete.

200. These fundamental changes in world economy and their impact on the international class struggle were reflected within the International Committee and, in the final analysis, led to the split. The basic difference in political perspective—between, on one side, revolutionary internationalism and, on the other, national opportunism—emerged clearly well in advance of the organizational split. In a letter to Michael Banda, dated January 23, 1984, North wrote on behalf of the Workers League: "No matter how promising certain developments within the national work of the sections may appear—such as our own experiences in various trade union struggles—these will not produce real gains for the sections involved unless such work is guided by a scientifically-worked out international perspective. The more the Workers League turns toward the working class, the more we feel the need for the closest collaboration with our international comrades to drive the work forward."[115]

201. The opposition of the Workers League to the national opportunism of the WRP was in theoretical alignment with social and economic processes that were already in an advanced stage of development, and which were about to blow apart the existing structures and relations of world politics. To the extent that large sections of the international cadre had been drawn to the ICFI in the 1960s and early 1970s, on the basis of the British Trotskyists' defense of the internationalist perspective of Permanent Revolution, the criticisms advanced by the Workers League, once they became widely known in the international movement, found overwhelming support. It was this that accounted for the relatively rapid political realignment that took place within the International Committee

---

115   *Fourth International*, Volume 13, No. 2, Autumn 1986, p. 38.

in the autumn of 1985. It established a new basis for the work of the international movement. The subsequent development of the ICFI was the conscious response of the Marxist vanguard to the new economic and political situation. The reorientation of the movement was based on a systematic struggle against all forms of nationalism, a reorientation that was inextricably tied to the development of an international perspective. All opportunism is ultimately rooted in definite forms of national adaptation. In the struggle against other tendencies and within its own organization, the ICFI reasserted the conceptions developed in their highest form by Trotsky—the primacy of the global developments of world capitalism over the particular manifestations in any given nation-state, and the primacy of international strategy over national tactics.

After the Split:
The Significance and Implications of Globalization

202. In the immediate aftermath of the split, the International Committee subjected the dissolution of the Workers Revolutionary Party to a detailed analysis. *How the WRP Betrayed Trotskyism 1973-1985* demonstrated that the crisis in that organization was bound up with its retreat from the principles that the British Trotskyists had previously defended in the founding of the International Committee and, later, in their struggle against the unprincipled reunification carried out by the SWP with the Pabloites in 1963. The International Committee then responded to Michael Banda's attack on the history of the Trotskyist movement, publishing *The Heritage We Defend: A Contribution to the History of the Fourth International*, by David North.

203. Having analyzed the historical roots and political origins of the split in the International Committee, the ICFI initiated a systematic examination of the changes in world economy that provided the objective foundations for the development of the class struggle and the building of the Fourth International. At the fourth plenum of the International Committee in July 1987, the following questions were posed: 1) With what new tendencies of world economic and political development is the growth of the International Committee of the Fourth International a con-

scious expression? 2) On what objective basis can the development of a new world revolutionary crisis be anticipated?

204. In its answer to these questions, the ICFI placed central emphasis on the "explosive growth in the activity of transnational corporations." It stated:

> The result has been an unprecedented integration of the world market and internationalization of production. The absolute and active predominance of the world economy over all national economies, including that of the United States, is a basic fact of modern life. Advances in technology associated with the invention and perfection of the integrated circuit have produced revolutionary changes in communications which, in turn, have accelerated the process of global economic integration. But these economic and technological developments, far from opening up new historical vistas for capitalism, have raised the fundamental contradiction between world economy and the capitalist nation-state system, and between social production and private ownership, to an unprecedented level of intensity.[116]

205. The International Committee also noted:

> The phenomena of massive transnational corporations and the globalization of production are inextricably linked with another factor which has profoundly revolutionary implications: the loss by the United States of its global economic hegemony, in both relative and absolute terms. This historic change in the world position of US imperialism, expressed in the transformation of the United States from the world's principal creditor into its largest debtor, is the underlying cause of the dramatic decline in workers' living standards and must lead to a period of revolutionary class confrontations in the United States.[117]

---

116 *The World Capitalist Crisis and the Tasks of the Fourth International: Perspectives Resolution of the International Committee of the Fourth International* (Detroit: Labor Publications, 1988), pp. 48-49.

117 Ibid., p. 49.

206. Another development, reflecting the breakdown of the post-World War II order, to which the ICFI called attention, was the escalation of inter-imperialist antagonisms. At that time, the rapid economic development of Japan was the most immediate, though by no means only, source of these new tensions. The ICFI pointed to the implementation of plans to establish a unified European market capable of challenging both American and Japanese capital. The ICFI also attributed revolutionary significance to the vast expansion of the proletariat in Asia, Africa and Latin America—the result of the international export of capital in pursuit of high rates of profit.

207. The development of transnational production and the global integration of finance and manufacturing dramatically undermined the viability of social and political organizations embedded in the nation-state system. Though the global integration of capitalism was creating the objective conditions for the unification of the working class, this revolutionary potential required organizations and leadership based on a consciously internationalist strategy. Without such a leadership, the working class would be unable to defend itself against globally-organized capital. As the ICFI explained in its 1988 perspectives document, The World Capitalist Crisis and the Tasks of the Fourth International:

> The massive development of transnational corporations and the resulting global integration of capitalist production have produced an unprecedented uniformity in the conditions confronting the workers of the world. The ferocious competition between national groups of capitalists for domination of the world market finds its brutal expression in a universal campaign by the ruling classes to intensify in their "own" countries the exploitation of the working class. The offensive of capital against labor is realized in country after country through mass unemployment, wage-cutting, speed-ups, union busting, slashing of social benefits, and intensified attacks on democratic rights.[118]

208. The changes in the form of capitalist production brought with them a change in the form of the class struggle:

---

118   Ibid., p. 6.

It has long been an elementary proposition of Marxism that the class struggle is national only as to form, but that it is, in essence, an international struggle. However, given the new features of capitalist development, even the form of the class struggle must assume an international character. Even the most elemental struggles of the working class pose the necessity of coordinating its actions on an international scale. It is a basic fact of economic life that transnational corporations exploit the labor power of workers in several countries to produce a finished commodity, and that they distribute and shift production between their plants in different countries and on different continents in search of the highest rate of profit... Thus, the unprecedented international mobility of capital has rendered all nationalist programs for the labor movement of different countries obsolete and reactionary.[119]

It was precisely these developments that constituted the objective foundation to which the growth of the ICFI was necessarily linked. This point was developed and emphasized in an August 1988 report to the Thirteenth National Congress of the Workers League:

We anticipate that the next stage of proletarian struggle will develop inexorably, beneath the combined pressure of objective economic tendencies and the subjective influence of Marxists, along an international trajectory. The proletariat will tend more and more to define itself in practice as an international class; and the Marxian internationalists, whose policies are the expression of this organic tendency, will cultivate the process and give it conscious form...[120]

209. The ICFI warned that the new forms of global production did not diminish, but rather intensified the danger of world war:

---

119   *The World Capitalist Crisis and the Tasks of the Fourth International* (Detroit: Labor Publications, 1988) pp 6-7.

120   D. North, Report to the Thirteenth National Congress of the Workers League, in *Fourth International*, July-December 1988, p 38-9.

The global character of capitalist production has tremendously sharpened the economic and political antagonisms between the principal imperialist powers, and has once again brought to the forefront the irreconcilable contradiction between the objective development of the world economy and the nation-state form in which the whole system of capitalist property is historically rooted. Precisely the international character of the proletariat, a class which owes no allegiance to any capitalist 'fatherland,' makes it the sole social force that can liberate civilization from the strangulating fetters of the nation-state system.

For these fundamental reasons, no struggle against the ruling class in any country can produce enduring advances for the working class, let alone prepare its final emancipation, unless it is based on an international strategy aimed at the worldwide mobilization of the proletariat against the capitalist system. This necessary unification of the working class can only be achieved through the construction of a genuine international proletarian, i.e., revolutionary party. Only one such party, the product of decades of unrelenting ideological and political struggle exists. It is the Fourth International, founded by Leon Trotsky in 1938, and led today by the International Committee.[121]

Perestroika and Glasnost in the USSR

210. The struggle within the International Committee between 1982 and 1986 took place against the backdrop of a deepening crisis in the Soviet Union and its Stalinist regime. The development of this crisis arose, paradoxically, from the immense growth of the Soviet economy in the aftermath of World War II. This expansion further eroded the viability of the national autarkic economic policies based on the Stalinist perspective of "socialism in one country." The increasing complexity of the Soviet economy posed with ever-greater urgency the need for access to the world economy and its international division of labor. The mounting economic

---

121   Ibid., pp 7-8.

problems of the USSR, particularly as the rate of world economic growth began to decline from the generally high levels of the first two decades after 1945, were exacerbated by the gross inefficiencies of the bureaucratically-managed system, which made a mockery of the claims to scientific planning. As Trotsky had insisted in 1936, quality in a planned economy "demands democracy of producers and consumers, freedom of criticism and initiative—conditions incompatible with a totalitarian regime of fear, lies and flattery."[122] Trotsky had also noted in 1935, "The more complex the economic tasks become, the greater the demands and interests of the population become, all the more sharp becomes the contradiction between the bureaucratic regime and the demands of socialist development."[123] The contradiction between the political and social interests of the bureaucracy and the objective requirements of economic development found particularly grotesque expression in the regime's morbid fear of computer technology. In a country whose citizens were required to register all typewriters and mimeograph machines, the Stalinist authorities were terrified by the political implications of the widespread use of computers.

211. Opposition to the Stalinist regimes in the Soviet Union and Eastern Europe rose steadily throughout the 1960s and 1970s. There were reports of major strikes in the Soviet industrial city of Novocherkassk that were suppressed violently by the army in June 1962. The sudden removal of Khrushchev from power in October 1964, his replacement by Leonid Brezhnev, and the clamp-down on the post-1953 de-Stalinization campaigns were a desperate attempt to uphold the political legitimacy of the regime. The trial and imprisonment of the writers Yuli Daniel and Andrei Sinyavsky, aimed at intimidating the growing dissident movement, served to discredit the regime, as did the later exile of Alexander Solzhenitsyn. The coming to power of Alexander Dubcek in Czechoslovakia in January 1968, the so-called "Prague Spring," further frightened the Soviet bureaucracy. The subsequent invasion of Czechoslovakia in August 1968 and Dubcek's removal from power deepened the alienation of significant sections of the working class and intelligentsia in the Soviet Union and

---

122   Leon Trotsky, *Revolution Betrayed*, p 235.

123   "The Workers' State, Thermidor, and Bonapartism" in *Writings of Leon Trotsky 1934-35* (New York: Pathfinder, 2002) p 246

Eastern Europe who had believed in the possibility of reforms of a democratic and socialistic character. In 1970, mass strikes in Poland brought
down the regime of Gomulka—who had himself risen to power amidst
mass protests in 1956. In the face of these challenges, Brezhnev sought to
assert a Stalinist orthodoxy that imparted to his regime an utterly sclerotic
character. Significantly, this period was also one that saw the flowering of
"détente" between the Soviet Union and the United States—a process that
came to an end in the late 1970s when the Carter administration shifted
toward a more confrontational policy, which was further developed by the
Reagan administration.

212.   By the time Brezhnev died in November 1982, the regime could no
longer conceal the signs of serious economic crisis and general social stagnation. Significant sections of the Soviet bureaucracy saw the emergence of the
mass Solidarity movement in Poland in 1980 as a warning that a revolutionary
explosion was possible within the USSR itself. Brezhnev's replacement, the
KGB director Yuri Andropov, sought to implement various anti-corruption
reforms to rebuild the credibility of the regime. He also instituted a crack-
down on alcoholism with the hope that this would increase the productivity
of Soviet industry. But these measures were mere palliatives. The basic problem remained the nationally shut-in character of the Soviet economy. At any
rate, Andropov, who was seriously ill when he came to power, died of kidney
disease in February 1984, just 15 months after assuming office. His replacement, Konstantin Chernenko, was another terminally ill Soviet bureaucrat.
He lasted only 13 months. Chernenko was succeeded by Mikhail Gorbachev,
whose crisis-ridden regime ended with the dissolution of the USSR.

213.   Gorbachev initiated a twin policy of limited expansion of domestic freedoms (glasnost) and economic reforms (perestroika). The central
aim of the section of the bureaucracy led by Gorbachev was to channel the
mass opposition that existed within the Soviet population behind policies
that would restore capitalism. Gorbachev was relying on the disorientation
of workers produced by decades of Stalinist rule. He also counted on political support from the petty-bourgeois radical left. This was the only political calculation in which Gorbachev demonstrated an appreciable degree
of astuteness. Nowhere did the phenomenon, which the bourgeois press
dubbed "Gorbymania", find such unrestrained expression as it did within
the milieu of the left petty bourgeoisie. Ernest Mandel, seeing in Gorbachev

the apotheosis of the Pabloite perspective of bureaucratic self-reform, proclaimed him to be "a remarkable political leader," a Soviet version of Franklin Delano Roosevelt.[124] Peering into the future through rose-tinged spectacles, Mandel outlined four plausible scenarios of Soviet development. Not one of these included the possibility of the dissolution of the USSR—an extraordinary oversight for an author writing only two years before its final collapse! Mandel's disciple, Tariq Ali, the leader of the Pabloite organization in Britain, could not contain his enthusiasm for perestroika and its initiators. He dedicated his book, *Revolution From Above: Where Is the Soviet Union Going?*, published in 1988, to Boris Yeltsin. His moving tribute declared that Yeltsin's "political courage has made him an important symbol throughout the country."[125] Ali, describing his visits to the Soviet Union, informed his readers that "I felt really at home."[126] The policies of Gorbachev had initiated the revolutionary transformation of Russian society from above, Ali asserted. There were those, he noted cynically, who "would have preferred (me too!) if the changes in the Soviet Union had been brought about by a gigantic movement of the Soviet working class and revived the old organs of political power—the soviets—with new blood. That would have been very nice, but it didn't happen that way."[127] Ali then offered a succinct summary of the Pabloite perspective, which combined in equal measures political impressionism, naiveté, and personal stupidity:

> *Revolution From Above* argues that Gorbachev represents a progressive, reformist current within the Soviet elite, whose programme, if successful, would represent an enormous gain for socialists and democrats on a world scale. The scale of Gorbachev's operation is, in fact, reminiscent of the efforts of an American President of the 19th century: Abraham Lincoln.[128]

---

124   *Beyond Perestroika: The Future of Gorbachev's USSR* (London: Verso, 1989), p. xi.

125   Tariq Ali, *Revolution From Above: Where Is the Soviet Union Going?* (London: Hutchinson, 1988), p. vi.

126   Ibid., p. xi.

127   Ibid., p. xii.

128   Ibid., p. xiii.

214. The appraisal of the Gorbachev regime by the ex-Trotskyists of the Workers Revolutionary Party was no less uncritical. Healy declared that Gorbachev was leading the political revolution in the Soviet Union. For Banda, the accession of Gorbachev represented the final refutation of Trotskyism. "If restoration didn't exist," he declared, " it would be absolutely necessary for Trotsky to invent it! The whole of Soviet history—during and after Stalin—testifies against this infantile leftist speculation and points in the opposite direction."[129]

215.   In opposition to these conceptions, the ICFI explained, as early as 1986, the fundamentally reactionary character of Gorbachev's economic policies. In its 1988 perspectives document, it wrote:

> As he seeks to implement his reactionary perestroika, Gorbachev implicitly concedes the failure of all the economic premises upon which Stalinism was based, i.e., that socialism could be built in a single county. The very real crisis of the Soviet economy is rooted in its enforced isolation from the resources of the world market and the international division of labor. There are only two ways this crisis can be tackled. The way proposed by Gorbachev involves the dismantling of state industry, the renunciation of the planning principle, and the abandonment of the state monopoly on foreign trade, i.e., the reintegration of the Soviet Union into the structure of world imperialism. The alternative to this reactionary solution requires the smashing of imperialism's domination over the world economy by linking up the Soviet and international working class in a revolutionary offensive aimed at extending the planned economy into the European, North American and Asian citadels of capitalism.[130]

216.   The glasnost reforms and the loosening of restrictions on censorship opened the floodgates for discussion in the Soviet Union on political and historical questions. The bureaucracy retroactively "rehabilitated" many of the old Bolsheviks, including Bukharin, Zinoviev and Kamenev,

---

129   Cited in *The Heritage We Defend*, p. 498.

130   *The World Capitalist Crisis and the Tasks of the Fourth International*, pp. 30-31.

and was forced to acknowledge that the Moscow trials were based on lies. However, the bureaucracy could never rehabilitate Trotsky, since his criticisms attacked the social interests of the bureaucracy as a whole. If these ideas were to achieve a wide hearing in the Soviet working class, it would severely threaten the plans of capitalist restoration. In 1987, Gorbachev insisted that Trotsky's ideas were "essentially an attack on Leninism all down the line."

217. The ICFI sought to bring the perspective of Trotskyism to the Soviet population, publishing a theoretical journal in Russian and organizing several trips to the Soviet Union between 1989 and 1991. Its work focused on clarifying the place of Trotsky in the October Revolution, the origins and significance of Trotsky's struggle against Stalinism, the political program of the Fourth International, and the nature of the crisis confronting the Soviet Union. The ICFI repeatedly warned that the liquidation of the USSR and the restoration of capitalism would have catastrophic consequences for the Soviet working class. Speaking in Kiev in October 1991, David North explained:

> ...In this country, capitalist restoration can only take place on the basis of the widespread destruction of the already-existing productive forces and the social-cultural institutions that depend upon them. In other words, the integration of the USSR into the structure of the world imperialist economy on a capitalist basis, means not the slow development of a backward national economy, but the rapid destruction of one which has sustained living conditions that are, at least for the working class, far closer to those which exist in the advanced countries than in the third world. When one examines the various schemes hatched by the proponents of capitalist restoration, one cannot but conclude that they are no less ignorant than Stalin of the real workings of the world capitalist economy. And they are preparing the ground for a social tragedy that will eclipse that produced by the pragmatic and nationalistic policies of Stalin.
>
> This is not a theoretical projection: rather the future which threatens the USSR is the present reality in much of Eastern Europe. In all the countries where capitalism has been or is in the process of be-

ing restored, the result has been a catastrophic collapse of the national economy.[131]

These warnings were completely vindicated by the actual course of events following the dissolution of the Soviet Union in December 1991.

The End of the USSR

218. The formal dissolution of the Soviet Union on December 25, 1991, 74 years after the October Revolution, confronted the International Committee with crucial theoretical, historical and political questions. The origins, social character and political destiny of the state that arose on the basis of the October Revolution had been a central preoccupation of the Fourth International since its founding. In countless struggles within the Trotskyist movement, dating back to the 1930s, the "Russian Question" had been the focus of intense controversy, often associated with bitter factional divisions. The question of the nature of the Soviet Union was at the center of the splits in the Fourth International of 1940 and 1953. In the immediate aftermath of the split of 1985-86, the issue of the class basis of the states established in Eastern Europe at the conclusion of World War II reemerged as a crucial historical and contemporary question for the International Committee. In one form or another, all the revisionist tendencies attributed to Stalinism a central and enduring historical role. In 1953, Pablo and Mandel predicted that socialism would be realized via revolutions led by the Stalinists, leading to the establishment of deformed workers' states that would last for centuries. In 1983, on the eve of the eruption of the political crisis in the WRP, Banda told North that the survival of the Soviet Union was a "finished question," and that there was no possibility that it would, as Trotsky had warned, cease to exist. Within less than a decade after Banda's declaration, the Stalinist regimes in Eastern Europe and the USSR had passed into history.

219. In the months that followed the dissolution of the USSR, none of the revisionist organizations were able to offer a credible assessment of

---

131 "After the August Putsch: Soviet Union at the Crossroads" in *The Fourth International*, Volume 19 No. 1 [Fall-Winter 1992], p. 109.

the significance of this event. Many of the Pabloite tendencies ignored it as if nothing at all had happened. Having believed so fervently in the political omnipotence of the bureaucracy, they could hardly bring themselves to acknowledge that the USSR no longer existed. Moreover, even those who were willing to admit that the USSR had been dissolved still argued that this did not necessarily alter the class character of the state. Even without the Soviet Union, Russia remained a "workers' state"! This remained, for several years after the dissolution of the Soviet Union, the position of Robertson's Spartacist group and of one fragment of the Workers Revolutionary Party.

220. The International Committee of the Fourth International, unburdened theoretically and politically by the sort of illusions in Stalinism that characterized the Pabloite tendencies, was able to make, in a timely manner, an objective and precise evaluation of the dissolution of the USSR. On January 4, 1992, the following assessment was made:

> In the aftermath of the events of the past month, which marked the climax of the politics pursued by the bureaucracy since the advent of Gorbachev to power in March 1985, it is necessary to draw the appropriate conclusions from the juridical liquidation of the Soviet Union. It is impossible to define the Confederation of Independent States as a whole, or any of the republics of which it is comprised, as workers' states.
>
> The quantitative process of degeneration of the Soviet Union has led to a qualitative transformation. The liquidation of the USSR and the establishment of the CIS is not merely a reshuffling of the letters of the alphabet. It has definite political and social implications. It represents the juridical liquidation of the workers' state and its replacement with regimes that are openly and unequivocally devoted to the destruction of the remnants of the national economy and planning system that issued from the October Revolution. To define the CIS or its individual republics as workers' states would be to completely separate the definition from the concrete content which it expressed during the previous historical period.[132]

---

132   David North, *The End of the USSR* (Detroit, Labor Publications, 1992), p. 6.

221. The role played by the bureaucratic strata in the USSR had far reaching political implications:

> What has occurred in the former Soviet Union is a manifestation of an international phenomenon. All over the world the working class is confronted with the fact that the trade unions, parties and even states, which they created in an earlier period, have been transformed into the direct instruments of imperialism.
>
> The days are over when the labor bureaucracies "mediated" the class struggle and played the role of buffer between the classes. Though the bureaucracies generally betrayed the historical interests of the working class, they still, in a limited sense, served its daily practical needs; and, to that extent, "justified" their existence as leaders of the working class organizations. That period is over. The bureaucracy cannot play any such independent role in the present period.
>
> This is true not only for the Stalinist bureaucracy in the USSR, but for the American bureaucracy in the trade unions. At our last Congress we stressed that the leaders of the present trade unions cannot be defined as a force which defends and represents, if only in a limited and distorted way, the interests of the working class. To define the leaders of the AFL-CIO as "trade union leaders," or, for that matter, to define the AFL-CIO as a working class organization is to blind the working class to the realities which they confront.[133]

The Struggle Against the Post-Soviet School of Historical Falsification

222. The dissolution of the USSR provoked within the bourgeoisie and its ideological apologists an eruption of euphoric triumphalism. The socialist nemesis had, for once and for all, been laid low! The bourgeois interpretation of the Soviet Union's demise found its essential expression in Francis Fukuyama's *The End of History*. Employing a potted version of Hegel's idealist phenomenology, Fukuyama proclaimed that the

---

133   Ibid., p 20.

weary march of history had arrived at its final station—a US-style liberal bourgeois democracy based on the unfettered capitalist market. This was the summit of human civilization! This theme was elaborated in count-less variations by gullible and impressionistic petty-bourgeois academics, always anxious to be on what they take to be, at any given moment, the winning side of history. The conclusion that was to be drawn from the collapse of the Soviet Union was that socialism was an illusion. "In sum," wrote historian Martin Malia, "socialism is a utopia, in the literal mean-ing of that term: a 'non-place' or a 'no-where' viewed as an ideal 'other.'"[134] The triumphalism of the bourgeoisie went largely unchallenged by those on the left who, up until almost the moment of the final collapse, had looked to the Stalinist bureaucracy as the guarantor of socialism. Indeed, they were no less convinced than Fukuyama and Malia that the demise of the USSR signified the failure of socialism. In many cases, the demoral-ized repudiation of socialism as a legitimate historical project stemmed from an unwillingness to examine their earlier premises and perspec-tives. Not a small number of those who were anxious to abandon and curse Marxism had no desire to confront the political issues behind the collapse of the USSR—least of all the Trotskyist critique of Stalinism. The question that they sought to avoid was whether there had existed an alternative to Stalinism—that is, whether the history of the Soviet Union, and of the 20th century, might have developed along very differ-ent lines if the political program of Trotsky had prevailed in the crucial inner-party struggles of the 1920s.

223.   The English historian Eric Hobsbawm, a long-time member of the Communist Party, explicitly declared that considerations of the pos-sibility of a different development other than that which actually occurred were inappropriate for a historian. "The Russian Revolution was destined to build socialism in one backward and soon utterly ruined country...."[135] The revolutionary project was itself based on an utterly unrealistic ap-praisal of political possibilities. Hobsbawm argued that it was pointless to

---

134   Martin Malia, *The Soviet Tragedy: A History of Socialism in Russia, 1917-1991* [New York: The Free Press, 1994], p. 23.

135   "Can We Write the History of the Russian Revolution," in *On History* (London: Weidenfeld & Nicolson, 1997), p. 248.

even consider an alternative outcome of the Russian Revolution. "History must start from what happened," he declared. "The rest is speculation."[136]

224. Replying to Hobsbawm's contemptuous dismissal of any consideration of historical alternatives to Stalinism, North stated:

> This is a rather simplistic conception, for "what happened"—if taken as nothing more than what was reported in the newspapers of the day—is certainly only a small part of the historical process. After all, history must concern itself not simply with "what happened," but also—and this is far more important—why one or another thing happened or did not happen, and what might have happened. The moment one considers an event—i.e., "what happened"—one finds oneself compelled to consider process and co ntext. Yes, in 1924 the Soviet Union adopted the policy of "socialism in one country." That "happened." But the opposition to "socialism in one country" also "happened." The conflict between the Stalinist bureaucracy and the Left Opposition, about which Hobsbawm says not one word, "happened." Inasmuch as he deliberately excludes, or dismisses as unimportant, the forces of opposition which sought to impart to the policies of the Soviet Union a different direction, his definition of "what happened" consists of nothing more than a one-sided, one-dimensional, pragmatic and vulgar simplification of a very complex historical reality. For Hobsbawm, starting from "what happened" simply means starting, and ending, with "who won."[137]

225. The fatalistic apologetics of Hobsbawm were a refined and sophisticated expression of a vast campaign of historical falsification that followed the collapse of the USSR. A major role in this campaign was played by ex-Stalinists from the former Soviet Union, who almost overnight transformed themselves into the most embittered anti-Communists. They endlessly proclaimed that the Russian Revolution was a criminal conspiracy against the Russian people. General Dmitri Volkogonov was only the

---

136   Ibid., p. 249.

137   *Leon Trotsky and the Fate of Socialism in the Twentieth Century*, World Socialist Web Site [http://www.wsws.org/exhibits/trotsky/trlect.htm]

best known of this type. In his biography of Lenin, Volkogonov—perhaps admitting more than he intended—acknowledged that the change in his own attitude toward Lenin developed "above all because the 'cause', which he launched and for which millions paid with their lives, has suffered a major historical defeat."[138] Among the "crimes" for which Volkogonov indicted Lenin was the January 1918 dissolution of the Constituent Assembly, an event in which not one person was injured. But this did not prevent Volkogonov, in his capacity as President Boris Yeltsin's military adviser, from overseeing the tank bombardment in October 1993 of the Russian White House, the seat of Russia's democratically-elected parliament. Estimates of the number of people killed were as high as 2,000.

226.   At its plenum in March 1992, the International Committee discussed the relationship between the development of the crisis of capitalism and the class struggle as an objective process and the development of socialist consciousness:

> The intensification of the class struggle provides the general foundation of the revolutionary movement. But it does not by itself directly and automatically create the political, intellectual and, one might add, cultural environment that its development requires, and which prepares the historic setting for a truly revolutionary situation. Only when we grasp this distinction between the general objective basis of the revolutionary movement and the complex political, social and cultural process through which it becomes a dominant historical force is it possible to understand the significance of our historical struggle against Stalinism and to see the tasks that are posed to us today.[139]

227.   The renewal of a socialist culture in the international working class required a systematic struggle against the falsifiers of history. It was necessary to educate the working class in the real history of the 20th century, to recon-

---

138   Dmitri Volkogonov, *Lenin* (New York: The Free Press, 1994), p. xxx.

139   "The Struggle for Marxism and the Tasks of the Fourth International," Report by David North, March 11, 1992, *Fourth International*, Volume 19, Number 1, Fall Winter 1992, p. 74.

nect its struggles with the great traditions of revolutionary socialism, including the Russian Revolution. In the aftermath of the March 1992 plenum, the ICFI launched a campaign in defense of historical truth to refute the claims of the post-Soviet School of Historical Falsification. Beginning in 1993, the IC initiated a close collaboration with Vadim Rogovin, a leading Soviet Marxist sociologist and historian. Under conditions in which vast sections of Soviet academia were moving sharply to the right and supporting capitalist restoration, Rogovin had begun working to rehabilitate Trotsky and the Left Opposition. In 1993, having just completed a book that examined the emergence of the Left Opposition, entitled *Was There an Alternative?*, Rogovin met for the first time with representatives of the International Committee. He had already been reading the ICFI's Russian-language *Bulletin of the Fourth International* for several years. He welcomed enthusiastically the proposal to conduct an international campaign against the Post-Soviet School of Historical Falsification. With the assistance of the International Committee, Rogovin, though seriously ill with cancer, completed, before his death in September 1998, six more volumes of *Was There an Alternative?*

228.   Based on its analysis at the March 1992 plenum, of the problems confronting the development of socialist consciousness in the working class, the International Committee expanded its work on cultural questions, seeking to revive the intellectual traditions of the Left Opposition, which had assigned to them immense importance. This outlook found its consummate expression in such works of Leon Trotsky as *Problems of Everyday Life* and *Literature and Revolution* and in Alexander Voronsky's *Art As the Cognition of Life*. Working within and building upon this tradition, the International Committee recognized that the development of revolutionary consciousness did not occur in an intellectual vacuum, that it required cultural nourishment, and that the Marxist movement had a vital role to play in encouraging and contributing to the creation of a more advanced, intellectually critical and socially perceptive environment. In a lecture delivered in January 1998, David Walsh stated:

> The Marxists face a considerable challenge in creating an audience that can grasp and respond to their political program and perspectives. To belittle the need for the enrichment of popular consciousness under the current conditions seems highly irresponsible.

How does a revolution come about? Is it simply the product of socialist agitation and propaganda brought to bear in favorable objective conditions? Is that how the October Revolution came about? We have spent a good deal of time as a party thinking about this in recent years. One of our conclusions has been that the revolution of 1917 was not simply the product of a national or even international political and social process, that it was as well the outcome of a decades-long effort to build up an international socialist culture, a culture which brought into its orbit and assimilated the most critical achievements of bourgeois political and social thought, art and science. The essential intellectual bases for the revolution of 1917 were established of course by those political theorists and revolutionists who had consciously made the end of capitalist rule their goal. But the streams and tributaries that feed into and make possible a revolutionary torrent are vast in number, a complex system of influences that interact, contradict and reinforce one another.

The creation of an environment in which it becomes suddenly possible for large numbers of people to rise up and consciously set about the dismantling of the old society, casting aside the prejudices, habits and learned behavior built up over decades, even centuries; prejudices, habits and behavior which inevitably take on a life of their own, with their own apparently independent powers of resistance—the overcoming of this historical inertia and the creation of an insurrectionary climate cannot possibly be conceived of as merely a political task.

We recognize that the all-rounded socialist human being is only a creature of the future—the not-too-distant future, we trust. But that is not the same thing as saying that there need to be no changes in the hearts and minds of masses of people before the social revolution can become a reality. We live in an age of cultural stagnation and decline, in which technical marvels are primarily used in an effort to numb and anaesthetize masses of people and render them vulnerable to the most backward conceptions and moods.

The sharpening of the critical faculties of the population—its collective ability to distinguish truth from lies, the essential from the inessential, its own elementary interests from the interests of its deadliest enemies—and the raising of its spiritual level to the point where large numbers of people will demonstrate nobility, make great sacrifices, think only of their fellow men and women—all of this arises out of an intellectual and moral heightening which must be the product of the advance of human culture as a whole.[140]

Globalization and the National Question

229.   Among the political consequences of the dissolution of the Soviet Union was the proliferation of nationalist and separatist movements demanding the creation of new states. Multinational states that had been maintained within the post-World War II geopolitical framework were exposed, in the aftermath of the Soviet collapse, to a resurgence of various national, ethnic, and religion-based communal tensions. In most cases, these tensions were exacerbated by the United States and the European imperialist powers in pursuit of their own geo-strategic goals. The breakup of Yugoslavia in the early 1990s, with all its horrifying consequences, was the outcome of the strategic objectives of American and German imperialism. Especially for the United States, the breakup of the old Union of Soviet Socialist Republics and the creation of new "independent" states provided extraordinary opportunities for the projection of American power into the Caucasus and Central Asia. And even within the borders of Russia, separatist movements, such as that which developed in Chechnya, were seen by the US State Department as potential assets in the drive for global hegemony.

230.   However, it was not only political considerations that underlay the intensification of communalist agitation. The development of globalization, the ICFI explained, provided:

> ... an objective impulse for a new type of nationalist movement, seeking the dismemberment of existing states. Globally-mobile capital has given smaller territories the ability to link themselves directly to the world market. Hong Kong, Singapore and Taiwan have be-

---

140 David Walsh, "The Aesthetic Component of Socialism" (Bankstown, NSW: Mehring Books, 1998), pp. 35-37.

come the new models of development. A small coastal enclave, possessing adequate transportation links, infrastructure and a supply of cheap labor may prove a more attractive base for multinational capital than a larger country with a less productive hinterland.[141]

231. The International Committee insisted that it was necessary, in the interests of the international unity of the working class, to take an extremely critical, and even hostile, attitude toward the separatist movements. The dogmatic repetition of the slogan, "The Right of Nations to Self-Determination," was not a substitute for a concrete historical, socio-economic, and political analysis of national demands. This was all the more essential at a time when contemporary national-separatist movements generally were characterized by socio-economic and political perspectives that were blatantly reactionary. Comparing national movements in different historical periods, the ICFI wrote:

> In India and China, the national movements posed the progressive task of unifying disparate peoples in a common struggle against imperialism—a task which proved unrealizable under the leadership of the national bourgeoisie. This new form of nationalism promotes separatism along ethnic, linguistic and religious lines, with the aim of dividing up existing states for the benefit of local exploiters. Such movements have nothing to do with a struggle against imperialism, nor do they in any sense embody the democratic aspirations of the masses of oppressed. They serve to divide the working class and divert the class struggle into ethno-communal warfare.[142]

232. Predictably, the petty-bourgeois radicals of the Spartacist League, opportunistically adapting themselves to a variety of separatist tendencies, proclaimed that "David North 'abolishes' the right to self-determination."[143]

---

141 *Globalization and the International Working Class: A Marxist Assessment*, Statement of the International Committee of the Fourth International (Oak Park, MI: Mehring Books, 1998), p. 108.

142 Ibid., p. 109.

143 Cited in *Globalization and the Working Class*, p. 109.

Aside from the patently absurd formulation of this denunciation, the Spartacist attack was based on a falsification of the attitude of both Lenin and Trotsky to the question of self-determination. At no time did they define the self-determination demand as a sort of promissory note which Marxists were obliged to redeem at any time and under all circumstances. Moreover, they never elevated this demand above the interests of the proletariat as an international revolutionary class. Just as Lenin, in 1913, carefully defined the different historically-conditioned types of national movements, Marxists were obligated to be no less exacting in their evaluation of the objective content of the self-determination demands advanced by one or another political organization. As the ICFI explained:

> It has often been the case in the history of the Marxist movement that formulations and slogans which had a progressive and revolutionary content in one period take on an entirely different meaning in another. National self-determination presents just such a case.
>
> The right to self-determination has come to mean something very different from the way in which Lenin defined it more than eighty years ago. It is not only the Marxists who have advanced the right to self-determination, but the national bourgeoisie in the backward countries and the imperialists themselves. From the end of World War I on, this "right" has been invoked by one or another imperialist power to justify schemes aimed at the partition of existing territories.[144]

233. The national-separatist movements embraced by the Spartacist League—in Bosnia, the Indian states of Kashmir and Punjab, Quebec and Sri Lanka—were precisely those in which the reactionary character of the self-determination demand found its clearest expression. In the case of Bosnia, the imperialist manipulation of the religion-based nationalism of a section of the population, the Moslems, served the interests of the wider campaign to dismember Yugoslavia. In promoting national separatism in the Punjab and Kashmir, the Spartacists chose to ignore the thoroughly reactionary character of these religion-based movements and, particularly in

---

144 *Globalization and the Working Class*, p. 112.

the case of Kashmir, their links to broader geo-strategic conflicts between the major national states in the region. As for Quebec, the national movement has for decades served as a means by which the conflicting interests of various sections of the Canadian bourgeoisie have been fought out. In relationship to the working class, the Quebecois ruling class has been no less ruthless than the Anglophone bourgeoisie in Ontario or Saskatchewan. Finally, the Spartacist promotion of Tamil nationalism represented a political capitulation to the separatist perspective of the LTTE (Tamil Tigers) and repudiation of the decades-long struggle of the Trotskyist movement to unify the Sinhala-speaking and Tamil-speaking working class in a common struggle against the Sri Lankan bourgeois state. Investing national movements with a mythic and supra-historical character, petty-bourgeois tendencies such as Spartacist choose to ignore the impact of the political betrayals carried out by the opportunist organizations of the working class in fomenting national sentiments among oppressed minority communities. In the case of the Tamil community, the growth of nationalist tendencies in the 1960s and 1970s was bound up with the political betrayals of the LSSP—above all, its entry into the bourgeois coalition government in 1964 and, subsequently, its participation in the drafting of a constitution, adopted in 1972, that institutionalized discrimination against the Tamil language.

234. The International Committee's clarification of the significance of the self-determination demand, and its struggle against bourgeois nationalism and its petty-bourgeois apologists, contributed immensely to the strengthening of the revolutionary internationalist foundations of the Fourth International. In the aftermath of the dissolution of the USSR and the immense political confusion generated by this event, the ICFI's analysis confirmed that a genuinely internationalist program for the working class could be developed only on the basis of the Theory of Permanent Revolution.

Globalization and the Trade Unions

235. At the same time as the Stalinist bureaucrats were transforming themselves into capitalist oligarchs, the former Labor and Social-

Democratic Parties of Europe and Australia were ditching their formal allegiance to socialism, becoming the vehicle for sharp attacks on living conditions and social programs. Bourgeois nationalist parties that had once been nominally identified, in one way or another, with socialism or national reform—such as the Congress Party of India—began to actively collaborate with global finance capital in imposing austerity measures and privatizing state industry.

236. The degeneration of the trade union bureaucracies, including the AFL-CIO in the United States, was one example of this international process. While many of the unions that made up the AFL-CIO had been formed in mass struggles that had led to real gains for the working class, the unions accepted the political hegemony of the Democratic Party and the profit system. During the ascendancy of American capitalism, the unions were still able to increase the living standards of their members on the basis of a policy of national reform. However, under the impact of globalization and the deepening crisis of American capitalism, this perspective became unviable. The policy of the trade unions assumed an ever-more openly corporatist character. Even the semblance of independence from corporate interests was abandoned. Throughout the 1980s, the AFL-CIO in the US had worked systematically to isolate and defeat strike after strike. The bureaucracy increasingly separated the sources of its own income from that of the workers it was supposedly representing. In this process, the bureaucracy assumed a social identity distinct from and hostile to the working class. Ritualistic references to the unions as "working-class organizations", which failed to take notice of the changing social nature of its ruling apparatus, became increasingly hollow. In reality, the unions were not "workers organizations" but organizations controlled by, and serving the interests of, a distinct petty-bourgeois constituency, alienated from and deeply hostile to the working class.

237. The 1993 Workers League perspectives document, *The Globalization of Capitalist Production and the International Tasks of the Working Class*, explained:

> The basic orientation of the old labor organizations—the protection of national industry and the national labor market—is undermined by globally integrated production and the unprecedented mobility of capital. The role of these bureaucratic apparatuses in

every country has been transformed from pressuring the employers and the state for concessions to the workers, to pressuring the workers for concessions to the employers so as to attract capital.[145]

238.   On the basis of an historical analysis of the role of the trade unions and their recent development, the Workers League concluded:

> The Workers League rejects tactical opportunism and trade union fetishism and does not counterpoise to the betrayals of the AFL-CIO bureaucracy a syndicalist perspective. It addresses itself first and foremost to the advanced, vanguard elements of the working class and seeks to educate as Marxists a new generation of workers, who have largely been cut off from the traditions of Marxism. Therefore it insists on explaining directly and bluntly to the working class the political character of its old organizations and the social forces which they represent.
>
> The Workers League does not ignore the unions or the workers in them. We do not hold the workers responsible for the reactionary character of the organizations within which they are trapped. Wherever it is possible, the party intervenes in these unions (as it would even in fascist-controlled unions) with the aim of mobilizing the workers on the basis of a revolutionary program. But the essential premise for revolutionary activity inside these organizations is theoretical clarity on the character of the AFL-CIO (and its associated unions) and brutal honesty in explaining the unpleasant facts to the workers.
>
> The Workers League rejects entirely the idea that the AFL-CIO, as the organizational expression of the interests of the labor bureaucracy, can be "captured" and turned into an instrument of revolutionary struggle...[146]

239.   The Workers League withdrew its demand for a labor party based on the trade unions. This tactical demand had been appropriate during a period when the unions had the support of masses of workers, and still

145   *The Globalization of Capitalist Production & the International Tasks of the Working Class* (Southfield, MI: Labor Publications, 1993) p 8.

146   Ibid., p 51.

functioned, if only in a limited way, as defensive organizations of the working class. This was no longer the case by the 1990s.

The Formation of the Socialist Equality Party

240. In June 1995, the Workers League initiated a process of transforming itself into the Socialist Equality Party. It was anticipated that this transformation would be carried out over a substantial period of time; for this process involved not merely a change of name, but the altering of longstanding forms of work and the development of the revolutionary socialist movement's relationship to the working class, within the United States and internationally. The transition from a league into a party was begun and developed in the closest collaboration with the sections of the International Committee of the Fourth International, which began to implement the same transitional process in the countries in which they worked. The transition from a league into a political party was determined by changes of a fundamental character, not only in immediate objective conditions, but also in the historical context within which the ICFI conducted its activity. The decision expressed the judgment of the Workers League and the ICFI that the discrediting and breakdown of the old mass organizations of the working class, rooted in the breakdown of the post-World War II equilibrium, had set into motion a process of political realignment by the working class on an international scale:

> It is the development of the contradictions of world capitalism and the class struggle as an objective historical process that determines the organizational forms within which our activity develops. These forms, and the relation to the working class that they express, bear a specific relation to the historic conditions under which they arose and initially developed. The formation of leagues, from the Socialist Labour League in Britain in 1959, the Workers League in 1966, the Revolutionary Communist League in 1968, to the formation of the Bund Sozialistischer Arbeiter in 1971 and the Socialist Labour League in Australia in 1972, was bound up with definite historical conditions and strategic conceptions of the development of the revolutionary movement of the working class.

The central strategical problem that confronted the Trotskyist movement in this early period in the development of the ICFI was the active and militant allegiance given by the most advanced sections of the working class to the mass Stalinist and Social-Democratic parties and trade unions.

The political activity of our sections therefore assumed, despite variations in tactics, that the starting point of a great new revolutionary reorientation of the working class would proceed in the form of a radicalization among the most class-conscious and politically-active elements within the ranks of these organizations. Out of that movement, in which the sections of the International Committee would play a catalytic role as the most intransigent opponents of Social Democracy and Stalinism, would arise the real possibilities for the establishment of a mass revolutionary party.[147]

241. The formation of the SEP anticipated a change in the relationship between the Marxist movement and the working class:

We must draw the appropriate conclusions from the collapse of the AFL-CIO and correctly formulate the new tasks of the party. If there is to be leadership given to the working class, it must be provided by our party. If a new road is to be opened for the masses of working people, it must be opened by our organization. The problem of leadership cannot be resolved on the basis of a clever tactic. We cannot resolve the crisis of working class leadership by "demanding" that others provide that leadership. If there is to be a new party, we must build it.[148]

The Significance of Equality

242. The selection of the name "Socialist Equality Party" expressed both a conception of the essential vision of socialism—the realization of

---

147 David North, *The Workers League and the Founding of the Socialist Equality Party* (Detroit: Labor Publications, 1996), pp 18-19.

148 Ibid., p 30.

genuine human equality—and an attitude of intransigent revolutionary opposition to the conditions of modern-day capitalism. In calling for the formation of the Socialist Equality Party, North stated:

> Objective conditions lead in the direction of revolution. But the development of revolutionary consciousness is not, as we know from history, an automatic process. The impulses generated by the subterranean contradictions of capitalism do not directly translate themselves into socialist forms of thinking. The response of the working class to a given objective situation is bound up with a vast complex of historically-given conditions. These may and, indeed, do vary from country. But in each case the Marxists must find the path to the minds and, I might add, the hearts of the working class.
>
> In transforming the league into a party, we must consider the form in which the crisis of the capitalist system reveals itself to the broad mass of working people. To put it most simply, millions of working people have experienced a protracted and ongoing decline in their standard of living. They live their lives in permanent fear for the security of their jobs, struggling to make ends meet as wages decline and prices rise.
>
> The dominant feature of American life is the widening gap between a small percentage of the population that enjoys unprecedented wealth and the broad mass of the working population that lives in varying degrees of economic uncertainty and distress...
>
> The deterioration in the economic position and social conditions of the working class is directly related to the technological revolution and the globalization of production that it has fueled. Under the regime of the private ownership of the productive forces, the working class is victimized by technology...
>
> The aim of our party should be stated in its name and in a manner that the workers can both understand and identify with. ...
>
> Briefly, in presenting this party to the working class, we must explain that its goal is the establishment of a workers' government: and by that we mean a government for the workers, of the workers and by the workers. Such a government will utilize the political power it intends to gain through democratic means, if possible, to reorga-

nize economic life in the interests of the working class, to overcome and replace the socially-destructive market forces of capitalism with democratic social planning, to undertake a radical reorganization of production to meet the urgent social needs of the working people, to effect a radical and socially-just redistribution of wealth in favor of the working population, and thereby lay the basis for socialism.

We will stress that these aims of the Socialist Equality Party are realizable only in alliance with, and as an integral part of, a consciously internationalist movement of the working class. There cannot be social equality and social justice for the American worker as long as multinational and transnational corporations exploit and oppress his class brothers and sisters in other countries. Moreover, there exists no viable national strategy upon which the class struggle can be based. The working class must consistently and systematically counterpose its international strategy to the international strategy of the transnational corporations. There can be no compromise on this essential question, which is the cutting edge of the socialist program. ...

... The demand for social equality not only sums up the basic aim of the socialist movement; it also evokes the egalitarian traditions that are so deeply rooted in the genuinely democratic and revolutionary traditions of the American workers. All the great social struggles of American history have inscribed on their banners the demand for social equality. It is no accident that today, in the prevailing environment of political reaction, this ideal is under relentless attack.[149]

The World Socialist Web Site

243. The establishment of the World Socialist Web Site in January 1998 marked a milestone in the history of the ICFI and the international workers' movement. It was the outcome of the development of the International Committee, in the aftermath of the 1985-86 split with the Workers Revolutionary Party, into a politically unified world party.

---

149   Ibid., pp. 31-37.

Moreover, the underlying conception of the WSWS—that the ICFI would play the decisive role in the political reorientation of the working class on the basis of Marxism—was derived from the perspective that motivated the transformation of the leagues into parties. The technological preconditions for the launching of the WSWS came in the form of the revolutionary advances of communication, which the ICFI had been carefully following as part of its analysis of the significance of globalization. It was consciously seeking ways to integrate the different sections of the movement in common collaborative work (including the early use of modems to send files across oceans and continents). It was highly attuned to the significance of the Internet. This revolutionary advance in global communications created favorable conditions for both the dissemination of revolutionary ideas and the organization of revolutionary work. For many decades the production of newspapers had played a central and critical role in the building of the revolutionary movement. Lenin had devoted a substantial section of his seminal work, *What Is To Be Done?*, to explaining the role of the All-Russian newspaper. Since its founding in 1966, the Workers League had published a newspaper. But its circulation was dependent on the number of party members physically available in any given location to organize its distribution. As long as there existed no viable alternative to the newspaper as a means of circulating its ideas, the Workers League and the different sections of the ICFI had to confront the limitations as well as they could. The development of the Internet created new conditions for overcoming old limitations and expanding the audience of the SEP and the International Committee.

244. The WSWS was not merely the product of technological developments. It was based on the accumulated theoretical capital of the world Marxist movement. Upon launching the WSWS, the editorial board explained:

> The World Socialist Web Site, published by the coordinated efforts of ICFI members in Asia, Australia, Europe and North America, takes as its starting point the international character of the class struggle. It assesses political developments in every country from the standpoint of the world crisis of capitalism and the political tasks confronting the international working class. Flowing from

this perspective, it resolutely opposes all forms of chauvinism and national parochialism.

We are confident that the WSWS will become an unprecedented tool for the political education and unification of the working class on an international scale. It will help working people of different countries coordinate their struggles against capital, just as the transnational corporations organize their war against labor across national boundaries. It will facilitate discussion between workers of all nations, allowing them to compare their experiences and elaborate a common strategy.

The ICFI expects the world audience for the World Socialist Web Site to grow as the Internet expands. As a rapid and global form of communication, the Internet has extraordinary democratic and revolutionary implications. It can enable a mass audience to gain access to the intellectual resources of the world, from libraries and archives to museums.

In the fifteenth century Gutenberg's invention of the printing press played a critical role in breaking the control of the Church over intellectual life, undermining feudal institutions, and fostering the great cultural revival that began with the Renaissance and ultimately found expression in the Enlightenment and the French Revolution. So today the Internet can facilitate a renewal of revolutionary thought. The International Committee of the Fourth International intends to use this technology as a tool for the liberation of the working people and oppressed all over the world.[150]

During its first decade of publication, the WSWS posted over 20,000 articles, covering a wide range of political, economic, social, cultural, and historical issues. Work on this scale has only been possible because the ICFI had accumulated over many decades an immense capital of historical experience. Moreover, its theoretical work has been deeply rooted in the traditions of classical Marxism, which strives to establish, on the basis of dialectical and historical materialism, the most precise and accurate alignment of subjective consciousness with objective reality—not merely for the sake of in-

---

150   http://www.wsws.org/sections/category/about/about.shtml

terpreting events, but with the goal of preparing the working class for revolutionary struggle.

The Explosion of Militarism and the Crisis of American Society

245. The WSWS demonstrated a level of insight in its analysis of the unfolding crisis of American and world imperialism unequaled by any other publication. What distinguished the analysis presented in the WSWS was its historical character, its ability to situate events in a broader context, and see through and beyond their surface appearance. On this basis, the SEP detected, amidst the displays of American military power, the contradictions that were eroding the foundations of the entire imperialist order. It insisted that the United States' repeated use of military power was a sign of weakness:

> The United States presently enjoys a "competitive advantage" in the arms industry. But neither this advantage nor the products of this industry can guarantee world dominance. Despite the sophistication of its weaponry, the financial-industrial foundation of the United States' preeminent role in the affairs of world capitalism is far less substantial than it was 50 years ago. Its share of world production has declined dramatically. Its international trade deficit increases by billions of dollars every month. The conception that underlies the cult of precision-guided munitions—that mastery in the sphere of weapons technology can offset these more fundamental economic indices of national strength—is a dangerous delusion…
>
> Indeed, the infatuation with the "wonders" of weapons technology and the "miracles" they promise is most common among ruling elites who have arrived, whether they know it or not, at a historical dead end. Bewildered by a complex array of international and domestic socioeconomic contradictions which they hardly understand and for which there are no conventional solutions, they see in weapons and war a means of blasting their way through problems.[151]

---

151   D. North, "After the Slaughter: Political Lessons of the Balkan War" http://www.wsws.org/articles/1999/jun1999/balk-j14.shtml

246. The analysis presented by the SEP related the eruption of imperialist violence to the deepening social contradictions of American society:

> The growing chasm between the privileged strata that comprise capitalism's ruling elite and the broad mass of working people denotes an objectively high level of social and class tensions. It may appear that this assessment is contradicted by the absence of militant labor activism in the United States. But the low level of strike activity and other forms of mass social protest do not indicate social stability. Rather, the fact that the last decade has seen so few open manifestations of class conflict, despite rapidly growing social inequality, suggests that the existing political and social institutions of the US have become unresponsive to the accumulating discontent of the working class. Established social organizations such as the trade unions no longer function even in a limited way as conduits of popular grievances. ...
>
> ... What the working class now requires is a new revolutionary international organization, whose strategy, perspective and program correspond to the objective tendencies of world economy and historical development.
>
> There are, we know very well, legions of pessimists who are convinced that there exists no possibility whatsoever of building such an international revolutionary movement. One might note that the most incorrigible of these pessimists are to be found precisely among those who not so long ago placed full confidence in the trade unions and believed deeply in the permanence of the USSR. Yesterday they were convinced that bureaucratically administered reformism would last forever. Today they believe with no less conviction in the eternal triumph of capitalist reaction. But underlying the giddy optimism of yesterday and the demoralized pessimism of today is a certain type of intellectual and political superficiality, whose characteristic features are an unwillingness and inability to examine events within the necessary historical framework, and a disinclination to investigate the contradictions that underlie the highly misleading surface appearance of social stability...
>
> Confidence in the revolutionary role of the working class and the objective possibility of socialism is not a matter of faith, but of theo-

retical insight into the objective laws of capitalist development and knowledge of history—particularly that of the 20ᵗʰ century...[152]

247. Subsequent developments, especially those which followed the strange and unexplained events of September 11, 2001, have substantiated the SEP's warnings of the global eruption of American imperialism. Neither the invasion of Afghanistan in 2001 nor the invasion of Iraq in March 2003 caught the WSWS by surprise. Its analyses have stood the test of time. Within 24 hours of the attack in Iraq, the SEP foresaw the likely consequences of the invasion:

> The 20ᵗʰ century was not lived in vain. Its triumphs and tragedies have bequeathed to the working class invaluable political lessons, among which the most important is the understanding of the significance and implications of imperialist war. It is, above all, the manifestation of national and international contradictions that can find no solution within 'normal' channels. Whatever the outcome of the initial stages of the conflict that has begun, American imperialism has a rendezvous with disaster. It cannot conquer the world. It cannot re-impose colonial shackles upon the masses of the Middle East. It will not find through the medium of war a viable solution to its internal maladies. Rather, the unforeseen difficulties and mounting resistance engendered by war will intensify all of the internal contradictions of American society.[153]

The Crisis of World Capitalism and the Tasks of the Socialist Equality Party

248. The crisis of American capitalism is only one expression of a general crisis of the world capitalist system, a process which the WSWS has analyzed in detail. The eruption of the so-called Asian financial crisis

---

152   Ibid.

153   "The crisis of American capitalism and the war against Iraq," http://www.wsws.org/ articles/2003/mar2003/iraq-m21.shtml

in July 1997, and the collapse of the dot.com bubble in the US, revealed the explosive contradictions arising from the creation of a global financial system and ever-increasing financialization of the American economy. As a report delivered by Nick Beams, the national secretary of the SEP in Australia, to a conference in Sydney in January 2000, noted:

> Over the last 10 years we have seen a series of deepening cri-
> ses in global financial markets. First there was the recession of the
> early 1990s which opened a period of corporate job destruction that
> has continued unabated, despite claims that unemployment levels
> are being reduced. In 1992 we saw the crisis of the British pound
> and the European Exchange Rate Mechanism and the crisis of the
> Scandinavian banking system. Then came the bond market crisis of
> 1994, followed by the Mexican crisis of 1994-95 and the emergency
> $50 billion bailout organized by the Clinton administration on behalf
> of the US banks. No sooner had the Mexican crisis been 'resolved'
> than it was followed by the so-called Asian financial crisis of 1997-98,
> which led to the Russian default, the bankruptcy of the US hedge
> fund Long Term Capital Management in September 1998, and the
> intervention of the US Federal Reserve to head off the threat of a
> systemic crisis of the US and global financial system. Of course the
> designation of these events as the Mexican crisis, the Asian crisis and
> the Russian default is something of a misnomer. What we are wit-
> nessing are different manifestations of a crisis of the global financial
> system. Just as gout first strikes at the extremities of the body before
> reaching the heart, the global financial crisis is now expressing itself in
> the events now unfolding in the United States.

249.   After the recession of 2000-2001, the US and world economy enjoyed a period of expansion, with some of the highest global growth rates
since the post-war economic boom. But this capitalist upswing was based
on increasingly unstable foundations, manifested above all in the growth
of debt in the US and the creation of a series of bubbles—stock market,
dot.com, property. The contradictions of capitalism erupted in open form
once again in the financial crisis of 2007-2008. A report by Nick Beams
explained in January 2008:

The financial crisis in the US and the expanded growth of the world economy, especially over the past seven years in the less developed countries, are not separate events, but different sides or aspects of a single process. ... The expanded growth of China (along with other countries) would not have been possible without the massive growth of debt in the US. But this growth of debt, which has sustained the US economy as well as global demand, has now resulted in a crisis. At the same time, low-cost production in China and other regions, and the integration of these regions into the world economy, lowered inflationary pressures. This process created the conditions for lower interest rates, thereby fueling the expansion of credit that has played such a vital role in sustaining the US economy and the world economy as a whole.[154]

250. Sixteen years after the collapse of the USSR, world capitalism is in a state of crisis, concentrated, above all, in the center of imperialism, the United States. As it entered 2008, the SEP drew a balance sheet of the objective crisis and the tasks of the party. It was noted that the extraordinary growth of social inequality over the last three decades "is rapidly approaching the point of open and violent class conflict."

The sclerotic American political system, administered by two political parties that serve as instruments for the implementation of the interests of the ruling plutocracy, is organically incapable of responding in any sort of credible, let alone progressive, manner to the demands of the people for significant social change. In the final analysis, the demand for social change, even of a reformist character, runs up against the unyielding determination of the ruling elite to defend its wealth and social privileges...

Regardless of who is ultimately nominated by the bourgeois parties and elected president, the logic of social and political developments is leading inexorably toward an intensification of class conflict. Moreover, the protracted deterioration in the social position

154 "The world crisis of capitalism and the prospects for socialism," http://www.wsws.org/articles/2008/feb2008/nbe2-f01.shtml

and living standards of the working class, its ever-decreasing share of the wealth of society, and the unrelenting intensification of its exploitation by those who own and control the means of production have laid the foundations for a profound change in the political orientation and allegiances of the working class. Those who fail to see or who even deny that the profound changes in economic life over the past 30 years have left deep marks in the social consciousness of the American working class expose not only their demoralized skepticism, but also their ignorance of history. Indeed, the absence of open social and class conflict during the past quarter century stands in sharp contradiction to the general pattern of American history. But this prolonged period of social quiescence, rooted in a complex and exceptional interaction of national and, above all, international economic and political processes, is now drawing to a close. The central task of the Socialist Equality Party in 2008 is to prepare in all aspects of its work—theoretical, political and organizational—to meet the challenges posed by the eruption of class conflict....

The Socialist Equality Party, in political solidarity with the International Committee of the Fourth International, anticipates with confidence the resurgence of working class struggles. We are convinced that the objective crisis of the capitalist system will provide the impulse for the upsurge of the American and international working class. But the coming upsurge will not automatically solve the problems of developing socialist consciousness.

As the initial struggles of the working class in recent months demonstrate, there remains an enormous gulf between the objectively revolutionary implications of the crisis and the present level of political consciousness. Objective conditions will propel the working class into struggle and create the conditions for an immense leap in consciousness. But it would be a mistake to underestimate the degree of struggle that must be conducted by the party to raise the political consciousness of the working class and overcome the reactionary influence of the bureaucracies, which, while weakened, remain a dangerous and critical prop of capitalist rule. Nor can we ignore the role played by myriad "radical" petty-bourgeois tendencies, which persistently seek to disorient the working class and maintain its subordination to "progressive" sections of the bourgeoisie. The influence of all these different political agencies of the ruling class can be overcome only by fighting for the assimilation of the strategic experiences of past revolutionary struggles and for an understanding of the implications of the developing crisis of world capitalism.[155]

The SEP, the ICFI and the Resurgence of Marxism

251. The instability of the world economy, the growth of global geo-political tensions, the eruptions of military violence, the deterioration of the social conditions of the working class in all countries, the increase in class conflict and the alienation of the broad mass of the people from the established political organizations indicate the approach of a revolutionary crisis. In the final analysis, the source of this widening pattern of disequilibrium is to be found in the incompatibility of the social relations and political forms developed by capitalism with the new global expansion and integration of the productive forces. This incompatibility can only be resolved and transcended through the conquest of political power by the international working class and the socialist reorganization of the world economy. The alternative is barbarism.

252. At the very center of this global crisis is the breakdown in the world position of American capitalism. The vast wealth and dominant world position that underlay American "exceptionalism"—i.e., the absence of a mass political movement of the working class—have been substantially eroded. American society is polarized along class lines to a degree unequalled since the social conflicts of the 1930s. But American capitalism is unable to offer the reforms that saved the system 75 years ago. The unending series of financial scandals and business failures have profoundly eroded public confidence in "free enterprise." The theft of the 2000 election, the lies told by the government to justify the invasion of Iraq, and the horrors of Abu Ghraib and Guantánamo have shaken the faith of the

---

155   D. North, "Notes on the political and economic crisis of the world capitalist system and the perspective and tasks of the Socialist Equality Party," 5 January 2009. http://www. wsws.org/articles/2008/jan2008/rept-j11.shtml

working class in the institutions of American democracy. The conditions for a radicalization of the social consciousness of the working class and an historic shift in its political allegiances are at an advanced stage. The United States is not exempt from the laws of historical development. It is entering into a period of revolutionary class conflict.

253.   Only a party that is unequivocally oriented to and based on the working class, is guided by the most advanced political theory, has assimilated the lessons of the past struggles of the international working class, and developed a program that proceeds from a scientifically-grounded appraisal of the objective tendencies of socio-economic development, can meet the demands of a revolutionary epoch. The Socialist Equality Party and the International Committee represent and carry forward a vast historical tradition. There is not another political movement that can, or would even want to, retrace its own history. The opportunist organizations—the Social-Democrats, the Stalinists, the trade unions and the Pabloite tendencies—have no desire to be reminded of their record of blunders and crimes. Nor do they wish to be constrained in the exercise of their opportunist maneuvers by the invocation of history and principles. The International Committee of the Fourth International is the only party that consciously bases its political work on great principles and, therefore, can present its history to the working class, without any gaps. It will attract to its banner the most determined, courageous and honest elements among the workers and youth.

254.   Celebrating the founding of the Fourth International, Trotsky declared in 1938:

> We are not a party like other parties. ... Our aim is the full material and spiritual liberation of the toilers and exploited through the socialist revolution. Nobody will prepare it and nobody will guide it but ourselves.[156]

255.   Seventy years later, the work of the Socialist Equality Party and the International Committee of the Fourth International invests these words with renewed significance.

---

156   "The Founding of the Fourth International" in *Writings of Leon Trotsky [1938-39]* (New York: Pathfinder, 2002), p. 93.

Read the World Socialist Web Site
www.wsws.org
*The authoritative international socialist web site
with daily news, analysis & Marxist commentary*

Join the Socialist Equality Party

For more information about the SEP, visit: www.socialequality.com
or if you wish to make an inquiry,
send an email to: sep@socialequality.com